Baby, You Can Do Better

A Standalone

Written By:

Tasha Marie

A Word

Wow, my first indie release! When I started my journey as an author back in 2017, I didn't know much about the literary world. I just knew I loved to read and write and I wanted to share my talent with the world. S/O to my former publisher but always my friend, Chyna L., for giving me the opportunity to shine as Ambitious Ink Presents' first author! Since then, I've written 9 books...9!!! Series and standalones. It may not seem like much to some but it's A LOT to me. I juggle mommy life, working full time plus battling depression and anxiety. It's not easy but I get the job done. I've read, I've watched, I've listened, I've learned and I've grown so much in these last two and a half years.

Much love to EVERYBODY who has pushed me to make this move independently. I can't wait to take my talents to the next level. Of course, to all my DAY 1 readers (you know who you are! *Drake voice*) as well as new ones looking for some DOPE new reads ... THEY'RE COMING! SORRY FOR THE WAIT! In an industry where new authors pop up every day, I greatly appreciate the continued support! TRUST ME, I'M WORKING and rebranding as well. I can only hope y'all still rock with me and my books in 2020 and beyond!

Enjoy this DOPE read and please be sure to leave a review!

xoxo Tash.

Synopsis

Have you ever looked alive but on the inside,
you were slowly dying? Yeah, me either.

This is my story and I'm not ashamed to run and tell. I want my voice to be heard and my pain to be felt. My name is Tahiry Monroe and my world went from rags to riches, glitz and glam to fighting for my life and crumbling from the abuse of a man. He promised me shopping sprees, diamond rings and trips across seas...but at what cost? Yeah, it's true. He was the boss. And me? I was just another pawn in his game. Look, you will remember my name and all the trauma too. I thought I was dead until help from the sweetest thug pulled me through. They say love is blind but shit, I can see clearly now. Are you ready to read my story?

Preface

"BITCH, I'MMA FUCKING KILL YOU! GET OVER HERE!!!" SLAP!

"Stop it!!! Heelllpppp!!! Somebody!!!"

"Shut the fuck up!!! Who the fuck you think you are?!" SLAP! "I hope that shit was worth your fucking life 'cause you bouta die today!"

"No!! Please...please...stop!!!" I was screaming at the top of my lungs, hoping somebody, shit, anybody, could hear me over the loud ass music playing in the house. Dolph was on a rampage and I just knew the day had finally come. I was about to die.

What started out as a kind of normal morning at home turned into drama. I was just about to start cooking up a big breakfast when Dolph came downstairs accusing me of fucking around on him last night because he found a condom wrapper in the bathroom trash. Like, what the fuck? Mind you, between the two of us, his ass was the fucking cheater. He probably forgot he did the shit. Dolph was tripping for real and I, of course, was the one suffering from it once again. He tossed my phone at the wall and the shit broke into pieces. He started to slap me around like I was a rag doll then dragged me down the staircase, not giving a fuck that my head was leaking from hitting the steps repeatedly. He continued to scream and shout at me like I was less than nothing. I could feel it in my soul, I was going to die at the hands of this man today.

"Dolph, what the fuck, bro?" My eyes bulged out of my head when I heard Dolph's brother, Snookie, yell out to him. Once again, he was witnessing some out of control shit, but for once, he actually spoke up. Snookie ran into the living room and grabbed him up.

"Leave us the fuck alone, Snookie!" Dolph hollered, pushing his brother off of him. The look in his eye was scary. I made eye contact with Snookie just as his crazy ass brother kicked me in the stomach.

"Ugh!!! Snookie...please..." I reached out for him with tears running down my face, hoping this one time he would step in and get Dolph off of me. Nope. This bitch ass nigga turned the other cheek and just shook his head as he left the crib. "Snookie!!!" Dolph punched me dead in the face. My nose instantly started bleeding.

"Shut the fuck up! Ain't nobody saving your ass, bitch."

He grabbed me up off the floor by my hair and proceeded to choke me out with his bare hands. The look in his eyes was dark and cold. He was gone. There was no coming back from this shit. I started kicking and gasping for air, trying to free myself from his tight ass hold. It was then I noticed he had dropped his pocketknife during the scuffle. I had to get to it somehow and someway. This shit had to end and it had to end today. The idea to try and poke Dolph's eyes out popped in my head so I did just that.

"Argh, stupid bitch!" He released me and I fell to the marble floor trying to catch my breath. He started screaming and kicking me in my back as I crawled across the floor to get the knife. He caught on quickly, but I was quicker. The second he reached for me, I whipped that shit out and sliced him across the forehead with the knife.

"BITCH, ARE YOU FUCKING CRAZY?! MY FUCKING FACE!!!"

I dropped the knife and started freaking out when I saw blood leaking from him as he ran to the mantle to look in the mirror. I stood up and froze for a second, unsure of what to do. A part of me regretted it and wanted to help him, then it was like something came over me. This nigga was just beating my ass, trying to kill me. Fuck him! Barefoot and all with just a nightie and my robe on, I bolted for the front door.

"TAHIRY!!!"

"Oh, God! Noooo!"

My heart was pounding harder than ever as I ran to the driveway. With shaky hands, I reached under the trunk for the spare key. Just as I heard Dolph open the front door, I jumped in the car and locked the doors. I fumbled with the keys to start the engine when this crazy ass muthafucka smashed the window in with his fist. Glass shattered all over me.

"DOLPH, LEAVE ME THE FUCK ALONE!!!"

"Where the fuck you think you going?" He growled as he reached into the car in an attempt to pull me out the shit. I threw the car in reverse so fast this nigga fell backwards. Once the car was in the middle of the street, I screeched off. I was frantic as all hell. Banging on the steering wheel, I started screaming my head off. I was sick of this shit. Looking in the rearview mirror, I was scared as shit that Dolph would follow me. To my surprise, he was nowhere in sight.

"Just leave me alone...oh, my God!" I cried. "Somebody help..."

It was so early on a Saturday morning that nobody was outside. Not that it would have even mattered. Nobody ever helped me. I had the worst neighbors. Everybody minded their business or maybe they were just tired of our shit because nobody came outside to help me this morning. Nobody ever came knocking on our front door. Nobody at all. I kept driving like a madwoman through the neighborhood with no set destination. My tires were steady burning rubber with every turn I took. I just had to get far the fuck away.

Breathing all heavy and shit, I looked up one last time in the rearview and sighed a breath of relief, thinking I'd finally escaped the craziness. It was over. That moment of relief quickly passed when a truck slammed into my car from the back so hard, I flew out of the windshield. I hit the pavement hard as fuck and heard the truck screech away. I couldn't move. I faded in and out of consciousness. I could feel myself slipping away.

"I'm sorry!" I cried aloud and rubbed my belly. "I'm so sorry. Mommy's sorry. I'm so, so sorry."

I tried. I tried as hard as I could to be a good woman. I tried to see past all the red flags attached to Dolph. I tried to deny what I already figured out. I tried to look for the good in every situation. I couldn't do it anymore. I had no more fight left in me. As I laid there ready to die and not even give a fuck, I thought back to the night I met Randolph Farrow and knew I should have just left well enough the fuck alone. But nope, I was blinded; blinded by his charm, his affection, his yearning for me and his money. Silly me.

One

FLASHBACK

"Shoulda never gave you my number, I did it with you. Shoulda never let you hit it, I split it with you. I regret it, you gots a fetish. You gots a problem, now it's a problem. Oh, no... skrr, skrr on bitches, I don't know these bitches. Did dirt on bitches, do it for fun. Don't take it personal, baby..."

"Ty, hurry up in the bathroom! I still gotta finish getting ready too! Damn!"

BANG! BANG! BANG!

"If you don't calm down..."

"Nah, 'cause we gon' miss the opening. HURRY UP!"

BANG! BANG! BANG! BANG!

"Girl, if you don't stop banging on my goddamn bathroom door like you ain't got no goddamn sense!"

"I'm sorry, Ms. Monroe. She's taking forever and a day."

SZA continued to sing her *Love Galore* while I hollered back. "I'm coming, damn! You cannot rush perfection!"

"Now what now? Uh, yes the hell I can!"

"Girl, relax. You know we gon' get there on time! Dang..."

"Both of y'all asses is getting ready to get kicked outta my damn house with this craziness!"

I continued to sing the hook. "Love, love, love, love, 'long as we got... love, love love, love..."

I laughed on the other side of the bathroom at my mother, Denise, and my best friend, Jalika. They both knew I took a long time in the bathroom when I was getting ready to go somewhere, especially if I was caught up singing a song. That was my thing. I could sing my ass off and the bathroom was my favorite spot to sing. Ever since I was a little girl, I loved to sing, my mother says. And for as far back as I could remember, she was right. I heard Jalika suck her teeth then bang on the door one last time as I wrapped my plush towel around my body. I swung the door open and she twisted her lips up at me.

"All done," I smirked and sashayed out the bathroom down the hall to my bedroom.

"Heffa. Fuck you doing, practicing for American's Got Talent or some shit?" Jalika slammed the bathroom door.

"Hater!"

My mother peeked her head out of her bedroom with a bowl of ice cream in her hand. "Where y'all going anyway?"

"Oh, you know...just out," I told her, keeping it simple.

"Mm-hmm...well, please be careful. If it ain't one thing, it's another in this damn city."

"I got you, Ma. Don't worry."

I closed my door and turned on my TV to Pandora to bump some music while I got dressed for the night. After a long week at work and helping my mom around the house, I was ready for a good ass night out. It was Friday and Jalika and I planned on hitting up the House of Blues to see Meek Mill's ugly, fine ass perform then hit the club for his official after party. I was thinking maybe I could get next to him and sing for a quick second. That would be everything!

As I picked out my outfit from the closet, I laughed to

myself thinking how fly I was about to look tonight. I was only five feet five inches tall, but I had definitely grown into my adult body at the age of nineteen. Although I wasn't a slim chick, wearing a size fourteen, I carried my weight beautifully. I had to thank God for blessing me with these curves because I could have been one of these bad body bitches, but I was shaped like a Coke bottle! Plus, my confidence was out of this world. I knew, regardless of my weight, I was the shit. My buttermilk complexion was blemish free, my hair flowed well past my shoulders and my deep brown eyes were big with a slight slant to them. My smile could light up the sky and my full lips stayed getting some kind of attention. I remember the days I was teased for having big lips and I hated it, but as I grew older, they grew on me. I was sassy, shy, and goofy as hell but serious when I needed to be. I had a loving spirit. My looks plus my personality made niggas flock to me all the time, but they were never about shit.

I was still a virgin so maybe that's why niggas always played with my feelings. I wasn't giving up the pussy or this neck...PERIOD! I toyed with my pussy often and could even make myself cum. I'd even practiced sucking dick with cucumbers on the low sometimes so I knew what I was doing...more or less. I wasn't about to let just any ol' body fuck. Niggas ran their mouths more than us females did. Shit was sickening. I wasn't one of these regular Boston bitches just sucking and fucking every nigga moving or every nigga with money. I talked to plenty of niggas over the course of high school and in the end, shit just didn't work out. I was waiting for somebody to show me something real and mean it. Or... maybe I was waiting for my prince charming or some shit. I couldn't call it.

See, even though I was an only child and the product of a struggling single parent household, I can honestly say mother did her thing on her own raising me. I was smart with a good head on my shoulders. I graduated from English High school in Jamaica Plain and I had plans on becoming the next big R&B sensation once I focused enough. My dreams were going to be my reality, okay! I dreamt of people harassing me on the streets for my autograph and even crying as I walked up on stages to receive awards. I wanted to work with all the greats. The only thing was, I procrastinated in major ways on perusing further action, but I was still young and living my life with plenty of time to get my shit all the way together.

I got dressed in a short black dress that hugged my body and purple thigh high boots on my feet. I rocked a simple gold necklace and studs in my ears I'd picked up earlier that day. Taking down my hair, I fingered through the wand curls, impressed that my quick weave came out so good. The Brazilian bundles I purchased from the beauty supply store surprisingly blended well with my real hair. I stepped back to admire my look in the mirror and just knew I would be turning heads tonight.

"And I see I'm still ready before your ass." Jalika busted in my room fully dressed and holding her clutch, giving me much attitude. Damn, near forty minutes had passed by. She stormed in my room twisting up a blunt.

Jalika was a slim thick Haitian chick. She wore a gold dress with black stilettos and her hair was slicked up with braiding hair added for a fuller affect to her ninja bun. I'd been teaching her some makeup tips I picked up on so her face was beat to the Gods. The big gold hoops in her ears, gold bangles on her wrist and sheer gloss completed her look for the night.

"Okay then, sis. I see you. I'm just about ready anyway," I told her as I finished applying my lipstick.

"You look cute too, bitch! I see the highlight on your face. You ready to be the baddest bitches to walk up in the House of Blues or nah?" Jalika stepped over to where I was by my dresser and bumped hips with me.

I kissed my teeth and grabbed my clutch. "Yeah. Come on, lemme request this Uber."

***

"Hold up, wait a minute, y'all thought I was finished? When I bought that Aston Martin y'all thought it was rented? Flexin' on these niggas, I'm like Popeye on his spinach. Double M, yeah that's my team, Rozay the captain, I'm the lieutenant..." The crowed sang along as Meek ended his set with this classic banger. Every bitch, including me, had lust in their eyes. After the four Patron shots, the two Coronas I threw back and catching contact from all the weed smoke in the building, I was feeling every bit of wavy. I didn't smoke so you can imagine how the room was spinning for me. I found myself turnt in my own zone as I had my hands up in the air. Suddenly, I felt the warm and strength of someone wrap their arms around my waist.

"This must be your shit, huh?" The bass in his voice had me shook and his breath was minty fresh.

I looked over my shoulders, wondering where this light skin dread head came from. He was fine as shit rocking a red "B" fitted, red Nike sweat suit and red Timbs. If he wasn't blinding me with all the damn red, the ice around his neck and wrists damn sure were.

I shook myself from his hold around my waist and said, "You already know." Then I flipped my hair over my shoulders to continue my vibe. Who the fuck was he to be grabbing me like that? Tuh...

"I'm that real nigga what up, real nigga what up. If you ain't about that murder game then pussy nigga shut up!" Meek was going off and the crowd was still rocking with him. Meanwhile, homeboy was still pressing his luck in my ear.

"So, you gon' tell me your name, right?"

"Damn, can't you see she's not interested, bruh?" Jalika snapped.

Before I could even get the full roll of my eyes to cuss hiss ass out, shots rang out not too far from where we were standing. I grabbed Jalika's hand then homeboy pushed us out the way and started busting his gun back.

"What the fuck?" I was confused as shit.

"Get them outta here!" Homeboy shouted to this tall ass, lanky, white boy who pushed us out the way. Everything was happening so quickly. Shit was crazy!

The whole building turned into chaos as everybody took off running and screaming. Same ol' shit. The violence in Boston was never going to end. Black people could never go out and enjoy the night without someone getting shot up or stabbed up. I was sick of this shit. Bullets were flying, muthafuckas were getting trampled and here was me and my best friend being whisked away by Superman or some shit. Through all the craziness, the white boy led us out of the mess through a side exit. Sirens could be heard in the distance as a red Bentley truck came screeching around the corner.

"Everybody good? Yo', where's my brother?!" The driver asked, hanging out the window with a blunt in his hand.

"Ladies, get in the truck please!" The white boy shouted at us, pushing us towards the truck.

I looked at him like he was fucking crazy. "Hell no!"

"The fuck? We don't even know you." Jalika snatched away and hugged me close. My fat ass was still trying to catch my breath from all that damn running.

"Where the fuck is Dolph?" The driver asked.

POW! POW! POW! POW! POW!

Now muthafuckas were shooting at the fucking truck. People were running and screaming their heads off, including me and Jalika.

"GET IN THE FUCKING TRUCK!" The white boy pushed us and started shooting back.

Homeboy from inside, who was all up on me, came running towards us, busting his gun into the crowd of people once again. We all hopped in the Bentley, including the white boy, and the driver sped off down the street.

"Yo' what the fuck was that shit? Who was them niggas?" The driver asked. "I keep telling y'all about-"

"Just drive, Snookie! Damn, bro! Y'all aight? Ain't nobody hit, right?" He asked, looking in my direction. "Kase, you good?"

The white boy wiped his forehead and nodded his head. "I'm good. Everybody good?"

I felt numb to everything at that moment and the goosebumps on my arms were serious. I couldn't shake this feeling. I wasn't necessarily scared but just shook up. Being from the hood, I done ran from a shooting a time or two before, but never that close. And to make matters worse, I was riding with the damn shooters!

Homeboy, who I now knew was Dolph, unzipped his Nike hoodie and placed it around my shoulders. "Aye, you aight? You good?" I was speechless, trying to wrap my head around what just happened. One minute I was jamming to my favorite Meek record and the next I was running for my life. I mean, what the fuck did he think? Dolph turned my face towards him and asked me again, "Are you okay?" The look in his eye was warm and welcoming, but I still didn't feel safe around him. I just wanted to go home.

I turned my head away from him and replied, "Take me the fuck home." I scooted closer to Jalika and eyeballed Dolph.

He kissed his teeth and mugged me back. "Aight. Well, where's that, beautiful?"

I folded my arms across my chest and flipped my hair over my shoulders then replied, "I stay over by Norfolk." I kept the shit simple. I didn't know his dangerous ass and as soon as we pulled up by *Only One*, I was hopping out and never looking back. I noticed Dolph was now looking out the window while fingering his goatee. He still kept his gun on his lap with his finger on the trigger. Crazy ass.

"I'mma just stay with you tonight, Ty." Jalika nudged me.

"Well, duh, bitch." I chuckled. We'd been friends for about five years now since we met in high school, and she was the main person who called me Ty almost always. Her ass came over my crib all the time and stayed the night, especially on the weekends. This was nothing new.

"So, what, y'all like best friends or something?" Kase asked us as he sparked up a blunt.

"I don't think that's any of your business!" I snapped.

"Yo', watch that attitude, for real." Dolph gave me the side-eye.

I raised my eyebrow. "Excuse me?"

"You heard what I said. Now you wanna be taken home and that's cool, but you not about to be snapping off up in my shit. You gon' get home nice and safely. And if you don't wanna fuck with a nigga afterwards then that's cool too," he stated matter-of-factly and grilled the shit out of me.

"Well then..." Jalika snickered. "I guess he told you."

Rolling my eyes, I replied, "Shut up. Wasn't your scary ass just crying?" Silence. "Thought so." I huffed and puffed, mad as shit that nigga just checked the fuck out of me. More so I was mad that I kind of liked it. The bass in his voice was crazy and the look in his eye was even crazier, but something about him turned me the hell on. I had to get the fuck away from him ASAP!

The rest of the ride was quiet as shit except for the trap music that played. Kase and Dolph smoked a fat ass blunt while Jalika laid her head on my shoulder. Snookie, the driver, just drove. And me? Well, I couldn't help but to steal glances at Dolph's fine ass.

When we pulled up to a red light by the restaurant, I said, "We can get out here."

Snookie asked, "In the middle of the street? Ma, you bugging."

"Nah, she wanna get out. Let 'em out." Dolph shrugged and I heard the locks.

I cut my eyes at him. "Come on, J." When I hopped out of the truck, it was just my luck my fucking heel broke. I collapsed to the ground, scrapping my knee and I was pissed the hell off. Tonight just wasn't my night. "What the entire fuck?" I cursed and shook my head.

Jalika rushed to help me up. "Damn, boo. You okay?"

"I'm fine…just fine," I mumbled.

"That's what ya ass gets for all the fucking attitude." I looked up and Dolph was standing in front of us with a big ass grin on his face. I cut my eyes at him and he started laughing. "My fault, ma. I'm just fucking with you. Why won't you let me take y'all all the way home?"

"You've done enough. Thanks." I snatched my clutch off the ground and started limping down the street. Jalika quickly followed suit.

"Aye, hold up…" Dolph came jogging behind us and snatched me by the elbow. Lord, this man just couldn't leave well enough the fuck alone.

"Come on, fuck them bitches, man!" I heard Kase shout.

"Don't pay him no mind. Lemme get your number. I'd love to make up for tonight." He ignored his friend and caressed my chin.

I frowned and looked over at Jalika who was standing next to me shivering her ass off. But the heffa was smirking at me and lifting her eyebrows as if to say "go for it." The fuck? Didn't she see what we just had to deal with? And we didn't even know these niggas! Looking back at Dolph, I shifted my weight to the other foot and squinted my eyes at him with my arms folded across my chest.

"Why should I give you my number?"

"'Cause I can change your life if you let me. But first, I just want your number." He licked his lips and pouted. "Please, beautiful."

For some reason, in that moment, he made me weak in the knees. I eyeballed him from head to toe and sighed. Shaking my head, I told him, "I'm probably gonna regret this but…fine." I watched him pull out his iPhone and I quickly rattled off my phone number. Then, I proceeded to limp away from his ass.

Dolph shouted. "So, what's your name?! And you got my jacket!"

"Oh well!" I hollered back and Jalika linked arms with me, cracking up laughing. "And it's Tahiry!"

"You ain't shit, Ty. He was fine as fuck."

"Girl, bye! We was running from bullets and riding with the shooters, crazy ass…" I rolled my eyes. I couldn't believe her ass.

"Well, bitch, you gave him your number anyway so…" She laughed and pushed me as we turned onto my street.

"Whatever. I hope his ass don't even call me either," I lied, secretly wishing he would hit my phone up tonight. Damn, maybe *I* was the crazy one.

We climbed the stairs to my house and I put my finger over my lips to tell Jalika's loud ass to be quiet. I knew my mother was knocked out trying to get some rest for work in the morning. We crept in the house and up the stairs to my room.

"What a night." Jalika fell backwards onto my bed.

"Tuh…a half night."

We both kicked our shoes off and laid the fuck down for the night. I couldn't sleep though. My mind was racing.

Two

Waking up in my bed to the sun shining into my room had me feeling like last night was all a dream. Did that shit really happen? Did I really run from bullets and ride with a shooter? Did he really ask for my number? Did my dumb ass really give it to him? I laid in bed staring at the ceiling, wondering what the fuck I was thinking. My mother would flip out if she knew what happened.

Dolph was fine as fuck though; caramel complexion, tall, muscular build like he spent his free time working out or some shit, luscious lips, grills in his mouth, long dreads, and a dangerous attitude. I knew he probably sold drugs for a living and it was evident he was into some gang shit or something violent. Still, he seemed to have a softness about him that intrigued me. Maybe that's why I gave him my number after all that shit. Or maybe I was just dumb and this was all going to end badly. Who knows? All I knew was I hadn't been able to stop thinking about him.

It was eight in the morning and I had to be to work by ten unfortunately. I was tired of this working for nothing bullshit, but I rolled out of bed anyway. My phone chimed on the nightstand beside me. I grabbed it and unlocked it. The text message read:

Dolph: Good morning, beautiful. I'm sorry about all that shit last night. You know how this Boston street shit works. You look like a smart girl. I ain't mean to put you in harm's way, which is why I wanted to see to it that you got home safely. You got a slick ass atti-

tude but I'mma tone that down. I wanna see you today, so when I call you, answer your phone.

"This nigga think he's running shit…"

I didn't bother to rely to Dolph's message but low key, I was excited he hit me up. It was a weird feeling. I looked at Jalika still knocked out, snoring her ass off in my bed. She sounded like a nigga slumped on a drunk night. I laughed and bounced up and down on my bed.

"Wake up, bitch!"

"Huh? Hmm…what?"

"Girl! Last night though." I snatched the covers off of her. "What the fuck was that?"

Jalika moaned and put a pillow over her head. "Damn, no. Ty, I'm tired as fuck. Move!"

"Dolph just texted me. He wants to see me again."

"Good for you." Jalika moved over and curled up under the covers.

"Bitch, you might as well wake that ass up. We gotta get to work anyway. Ugh, I've been up thinking about last night for like an hour anyway. Come on!"

"Come on what? I'm tryna sleep! I'm calling out."

"What? Stop playing. Wake ya ass up, J!!" I started bouncing up and down on the bed again. I knew it would annoy the hell out of her. "Should I let him see me or not? I'm low key excited."

"Well, shit, go see him and get the energy out on the dick! Bounce on that! Get out!!!" Jalika threw a pillow at me and started laughing.

"Fuck you!"

"No, bitch. Fuck him! Damn...ugh! See, I'm up now. The fuck." She frowned at me and rolled her eyes.

"Yes, finally. So you think I should give him the time of day?"

She stretched and yawned. "I mean, y'all would look cute as fuck together. He seems a little too hood and you're one feisty bitch but who knows? He just might be able to tame your ass. Now, his white friend, mmmm!" Jalika smirked at me. "Now that one can get the business."

I laughed and looked at my best friend like she was crazy as hell. "Girl, what? A white boy?"

"Don't hate. I mean, you know I love 'em chocolate, but that nigga was dipped in white chocolate so that's cool too. He smelled good as shit. Yeah, he could get it."

"Girl, what nigga ain't you giving the pussy to?" I laughed and cut my eyes at her.

"Shut up! I can't help it if my pussy is never satisfied. But that nigga right there, he gon' get this work." She stuck her tongue out at me. "I would love to see him again."

"I'm sure, heffa."

I climbed off my bed and walked over to my closet to pick out my black clothes that were required for work. Macy's Downtown was my place of employment and had been for over a year now since I graduated. Although I hated working, especially retail, I knew wasn't nobody else going to buy me shit or help my mother with the bills. I had to do what I had to do.

A knock came at my door and in walked my mother, dressed and ready to go. She worked five days a week at Bank of America in Dudley for over ten years now as a bank teller. She picked up working Saturdays doing housekeeping at a hotel in Fenway when the shitty ass landlord went up on the rent two months ago. Bills were stacking up and some more shit. Yeah, the struggle was kind of real. I knew my mother was tired of doing so much but she always kept her head up. The rent in Boston was way too high, but it seemed like nothing was going to change it. So of course I worked full time at Macy's and threw her some money every other week from my sorry ass paycheck.

"I heard y'all asses creep back in here last night. How was the night?" My mother eyeballed us. Jalika and I were both nineteen and I was turning twenty in a few weeks, so she couldn't really say much, but my mother had an opinion about every single thing in life.

"It was good, Ms. Monroe. We went-"

"To a party. It was fun and nobody got hurt, Ma." I interrupted Jalika to assure my mother with a smile on my face. I wasn't about to tell her we went to a ratchet ass concert and then hopped in the truck with some shooting ass niggas. Jalika woulda spilled all the tea for no damn reason, amped as hell to share the excitement.

"Hmmm, well apparently there was some rap show last night. Two people were shot and one died in the hospital. Y'all wouldn't know anything about that, right?" She asked us but looked directly at me.

Jalika and I both shook our heads and replied, "No."

I added, "That's crazy though. You know something's always happening these days, Ma." I went back to picking out my work clothes in the closet to avoid her heavy stare.

"Alright, well that's good. I'm glad y'all had a good time and made it back safely," my mother stated and pulled her little purse over her shoulder. "I'm off to work. I'll be back later. You going to work this morning, right? I could use a little extra this month."

Nodding my head, I told her, "Yeah, Ma. I got you."

"And Jalika, honey, please check in with your grand-mother so she's not blowing my phone up all day looking for your ass."

Jalika laughed. "Okay, I will. Thank you for letting me stay over last night."

"Girl, you never go home anyway. Bye!" My mother shut my bedroom door and clicked clacked her way down the hall.

"Your mother is hilarious."

"She's right though, J. You ain't never home, leaving grams all alone worrying about your ass."

Jalika was the turn up queen and was always down for whatever. We'd been best friends since freshman year of high school. She even worked with me at Macy's, but unlike me, she didn't have her mother around to help guide her decisions. I wasn't perfect by far and although I loved her like a sister, Jalika was a hot ass mess. She told me the story of how she was raised by her grandmother when her mother left her on the stoop one day to chase after a man in Texas. She was only seven years old then. When we met in high school at the age of fourteen, she was already smoking weed, fucking niggas and boosting clothes. In recent times, her grandmother was getting old as hell and suffering from cancer, but she was never home to take care of the lady. Grams stayed getting on Jalika's back about getting her life together before she passed on and as the months went by, I started doing the same. But as the saying goes, you could lead the horse to water but you couldn't make her drink it.

Jalika hopped out of my bed and started twerking. "I'm grown as fuck! She'll be aight, sis."

I tossed a pillow at her. "Don't be popping that last night pussy over this way! Move, we gon' be late for work, bitch!"

***

Today was one of those days I was wishing I randomly got rich as fuck and could tell this lame ass job to kiss all of my fat ass! I swear, I wasn't built to work. I needed to be one of these bitches in the hood books I read sometimes. You know, living lavish and driving fancy cars. Macy's was for the birds. Plus, Jalika worked in the kids department all the way downstairs from me. We didn't even take our lunch break at the same time so work pretty much sucked all the time. Working in retail barely paid for shit and after I got my hair and nails done, bought some cute clothes and gave my mother money, I was left with bullshit ass change until the next payday. Whoever invented bi-weekly pay needed their ass beat. Shit was sad as fuck and I was ready for a change already.

Saturdays in Macy's were always hectic and I was feeling every bit of the Patron shots from last night. I barely got to work on time fucking around with Jalika this morning so I didn't even have breakfast. A bitch was going through it right now. Just the thought of liquor had my ass wanting to run to the bathroom, but nope. Here I was trying to be a good sales associate. I worked in the Men's Department with a bitchy ass manager named Jordana who probably needed dick in her life more than I did. I knew she couldn't wait to get the perfect opportunity to fire me or for me to up and quit, but mama ain't raise no fool. I was going to rough it out until something better came along.

I finished ringing up this old, perverted looking ass nigga and handed him his Macy's bag. "Thank you for shopping with Macy's. Have a nice day." I barely wanted to say anything to him. His ass was drooling over me like nobody's business and he looked old enough to be my damn granddaddy. Ugh, I hated that creepy feeling.

"I sure will have a nice day, darling. Mmm...you so fine. Bye, bye." He winked at me and walked off.

Rolling my eyes, I found myself scrolling on my phone discreetly so I wouldn't be seen on camera. My notifications were lit on Instagram from my pictures and videos at Meek's show last night.

"So, you gon' read my message and not respond, huh?"

I was so caught up in my phone that I didn't even peep Dolph approaching my register. The nigga had me speechless for a second. He had that whole thuggish appeal to him, rocking a plain white, V-neck, short-sleeved shirt, grey sweats and black Jordans on his feet. He was tatted up from what I could see and the smell of his cologne made me weak in the knees. I just couldn't find the words that were stuck in the back of my throat.

"Um, hello? Cat got ya slick ass tongue today?" He said with a smirk.

I shook this weird feeling off and put my phone back under the register. "I was just...never mind. How did you know where I work? Are you stalking me?" I raised an eyebrow.

Dolph laughed. "Don't flatter yourself, beautiful. I was actually picking up something and I noticed you standing here." He looked around. "Didn't picture you working retail though."

I lowered my head in slight embarrassment and mumbled, "Yeah, whatever. How can I help you, sir?"

"You can start by letting me rescue you from work today. I'd love to kick it with you, Tahiry." He licked his lips at me. Them shits had me in a trance.

I cleared my throat, shook that shit off again and said, "Just call me Ty. And um, kick it with me for what? So I can run from some more bullets? Thanks but no thanks." I noticed a customer approaching my register. "Excuse me. I have work to do."

Dolph eyeballed me like he wanted to say something slick but instead, he slid to the side and waited patiently for me to ring the customer up. When I was done, he came back over to me and leaned over the counter.

"Why you so mean? I like you and I think you like me too."

"Like you? I don't even know you."

"Yeah, but you wanna get to know me. I can tell." He caressed my hand and then locked his fingers with mine. "So, what's good? Give me a chance to change your life."

I squinted my eyes at him. "Change my life how?"

"In a lot of ways, but I just wanna take you out first to make up for last night." Then he hit me with the same line that got me in the first damn place. He smiled at me with that nice ass grill of his and said, "Please, beautiful."

I hesitated for a moment or two, really contemplating what I was going to do. On one hand, I didn't want to be at work anyway, but I knew I needed the money. Then, on the other hand, Dolph had me curious to see what he was all about aside from the drama. He seemed to have a genuineness underneath the thug appeal. My mind was going crazy with different thoughts. It was like I had the devil on one shoulder and an angel on the other. *What the hell, Ty? You're single as a dollar bill! What's the harm in going out with a nigga? Ugh, your mother would never approve though. He's too hood. He's dangerous. But damn he's fine as shit. Go for it. What about work? You know you broke. Fuck it. It's just one shift you're missing. Go!*

"Alright. Fine. Where we going?"

Dolph winked at me and replied, "You let me take care of that. Meet me outside Burger King in twenty minutes." He kissed my hand and I watched him walk his fine ass away.

Slipping my phone into my back pocket, I left the register and approached the dressing room. Tapping my older coworker Angie on the shoulder, I told her to tell Jordana I was feeling sick and had to leave. Angie she was already hip that I just wanted to skip out of work. She smirked at me.

"Uh huh, I remember being young once, Ty. Have fun. I got you, girl."

I smiled. "Thanks, Angie. See you next week." I never left out of work so fast. Shit was crazy. I was so excited to see what this dangerous ass nigga had in store for me. I grabbed my phone and dashed downstairs to the locker room. I quickly changed back into the thick. comfy leggings, long sleeved sweater and Uggs I'd worn to work then dipped out the side door. This nervous feeling kicked in and I had to call my best friend.

"Bitch, what you mean you just left work? And without me? You ain't shit! You knew I wanted see the white boy, Ty."

As I walked out of Macy's to go meet Dolph, I rolled my eyes and listened to Jalika bitch and moan in my ear about me ditching the rest of my shift. I knew she would cuss my ass out so I was prepared for it. "Look, heffa, I don't know what came over me, but I'mma see what's up with him. Most likely we can all link later and do something," I told her, not really sure.

Jalika sighed into the phone and I could picture her face all screwed up. "Aight. Yeah, that's cool. Have fun and be safe with that nigga. Call me."

"You already know, bitch. Later!"

I ended the call and waited on the corner outside of Burger King by Park Street station. Dolph said he was parked out front but I didn't see any car. I couldn't help but bite my nails nervously. What the fuck was I thinking? He probably played me and my ass played along. I checked my face using the camera on my iPhone just as I heard a horn beep. Cars flew down Tremont Street, but it definitely wasn't hard to notice that fly ass red Bentley truck pulling up.

The back window rolled down and Dolph's face lit up like

a Christmas tree as he looked at me. "What you waiting on, beautiful? Let's ride!" He hollered at me with a wide grin.

"Oh my God! Is that Dolph?"

"Bitch, move! You knew I been wanted to talk to him!"

These two thirsty ass females damn near pushed me down as I started to make my way across the street. Cars beeped at them and I shook my head in disbelief watching these bitches damn near kill themselves to get to Dolph.

Snookie hopped out the front seat with the quickness to stop all the shit. "Aight, aight. Back y'all ratchet asses up!"

I started cracking up laughing when I got to the truck. Dolph wasn't paying them any mind when he hopped out of the back and pulled me into him. I heard them bitches suck their teeth as he laid a kiss on me so deeply it shook me to my core. Who did this nigga think he was to be kissing me? I couldn't front though, I loved that shit. I could feel the envious stares from the chicks next to me. I was shocked as fuck that he did that and my panties instantly got moist.

Dolph hugged me close and barked, "Y'all heard the man... back y'all ratchet asses up! Yo', bro, let's dip, man."

"So what, is this ya girl or something, Dolph?"

"Tuh, I didn't know you like big girls. You can do better than that."

"Much better."

"Period!"

Mind you, these bitches were ugly as hell! Only thing they had on me was slim figures and cute clothes, but I wasn't about to let no ugly bitch punk me, especially in front of his ass. I had to do something. "Ohhh, you bitches tried it!" I don't know what came over me, but I punched both of them bitches in the face and they dropped to the sidewalk.

Dolph pulled me back immediately. "Damn, Ty!"

A transit police officer came running right over with his scary looking ass. He shouted, "Whoa, whoa! What's going on here?!"

Dolph and Snookie immediately pulled out their guns and aimed it at the dude. Dolph yelled back, "Back your rent a cop ass up!" At this point, we were all drawing unnecessary attention to ourselves.

The transit officer threw his hands up, looking scared as shit and Snookie shouted, "Get in the truck!" He snatched me up then threw me in the back of the Bentley and Dolph climbed in right after me.

"Pull off, bro!" He was laughing his ass off.

My hand was killing me, but the adrenaline rush helped me out of that nervous feeling of being around him. "Dumb bitches..." I sucked my teeth.

He kissed my cheek. "You wild, girl! Lemme find out you out here fighting for ya man already."

"You definitely didn't look like you had that in you, Tahiry. You go girl!" Snookie laughed and cheered me on from the driver's seat as he sped off down Tremont.

"My man?" I turned to Dolph with an eyebrow raised while still massaging my aching hand.

He cut his eyes at me. "Cut that shit. You here, right? You just left work for me, right? Aight then, you fucking with me." Dolph leaned back and pulled me onto his lap then caressed my hand. "Nah, but for real, you good though?"

Nodding my head, I replied, "Yeah, I'm fine."

"I see that much." He smirked then got serious on me

quickly. "On dawgs, I done had bitches come and go, Tahiry. I see something in you that I'm tryna lock down. You're special." He cupped my chin. "Just let me show you what I can do for you and how I can make you feel. You wanna feel good, right?" He started rubbing my thighs and I got chills down my spine. I closed my eyes when I felt his lips on my neck and a soft moan escaped my lips. I kept wondering why this felt so damn good. This felt too right. Everything just felt right. My head turned slightly when I heard this loud noise and noticed it was black shutters sliding over to give us privacy in the back seat. Snookie blasted *The Chase* by Duffle Bag Trappy. That was my shit.

Dolph pulled his lips away from my neck and demanded, "Lay back."

Keeping my eyes on his, I did as I was told and the nerves in my belly were going crazy as fuck. What the hell was about to go down? Was he going to try to fuck me? Was I going to let him? He locked eyes with me and licked his lips as he pulled down my leggings. I was a clean bitch, but I couldn't help but kick myself mentally for not shaving this morning. It had been about three days and you know pussy hairs grew back within seconds! I swear to God, my heart was pounding as I covered my eyes with my hands. I couldn't believe how open I was being with this nigga already. I felt like I was under a trance.

"Look at me." The tone of Dolph's voice turned me the hell on. My clit was throbbing. I moved my hands and shyly looked down at him. "You gon' lemme make you feel good?" He leaned up to kiss my lips and our tongues started dancing again.

"What about...?" I motioned towards the driver's seat.

He ignored me and placed a finger to my lips before disappearing between my legs. He slid my panties to the side and I felt the warmth of his tongue part my pussy lips. I had to pinch myself to see if I was dreaming or not because this could not be happening right now. Was I really letting this nigga lick on my pussy? Dolph's tongue made soft circular motions on my clit. I looked down at him and he winked at me before really going in on my shit. He started making love to my pussy with his mouth. The kissing, the sucking, the licking and the nibbling had me arching my back and grilling his dreads.

I moaned loudly, "Dolph...!" Something came over me and I started grinding my pussy in his face. He gripped my waist and focused on my clit. My legs started shaking and my eyes got watery.

Was I crying? Was I dying and going to heaven? Shit, I couldn't call it. All I knew was this was a first for me and the feeling was everything. I was moaning my ass off, about to lose my fucking mind in the back seat. I didn't even care if Snookie heard me now. I didn't care about shit except the way Dolph was making me feel. He placed his finger in my mouth and this voice in the back of my mind told me to suck on it so I did. He groaned and really went Tasmanian devil on my pussy.

"Shiiiit, Dolph ..." I was trying to run from his tongue now. I could feel myself about to cum and it was going to be a big one. *Lord help me!*

"Cum on my tongue, baby. Cum for me," Dolph whispered against my pussy before dipping his tongue back all up in it.

His wish was my command. "Fuuucckkkk...." The hot tears poured from my eyes as I creamed all in his mouth. Fuck just my legs, my whole damn body was trembling from head to toe. My ears were ringing. My nipples were hard. My toes were curled the fuck up in my Uggs. I struggled to breathe and some more shit. Dolph slurped my pussy clean like it was Sunday dinner at grandma's house, then he kissed along the inside of my thighs, chuckling a little bit.

"You taste so fucking good, ma. Mmm... I knew you would. Goddamn..." I heard him groan and he bit the inside of my thigh before sucking on it. I quivered with pleasure. That shit felt so good.

Just then, there was a tap on the shutter and Snookie shouted over the music, "We here, bro!"

Shit. I'd really forgotten we were on our way somewhere. Dolph leaned up and kissed my lips, sucking on my bottom lip then asked me, "You good?"

My eyes fluttered a few times and I swallowed hard before replying, "Y-yeah...I think so. Shit..." I struggled to sit back up.

He laughed. "I got you. A nigga ain't never did that to you before, huh?" He helped me fix my clothes then gave me another kiss. I lowered my head in embarrassment. I mean, damn, here he was all experienced and shit. I was really a little ass girl when I thought about it. He lifted my head. "Stop that. Don't be ashamed. Understand me? I'mma make sure you feel good all the time. I promise you. I don't wanna hurt you." This nigga was doing something to me already. I couldn't call it but it felt good. I watched as Dolph reached into his pockets and handed me a wad of money. My eyes got wide as shit! He told me, "Aight, so you gon' go get ya hair and nails done at this salon, and I'll be back in like two hours to scoop you."

"What? Where you going?"

"To pick up our clothes and shit for later and make sure everything's all set." He winked at me.

"Later? Dolph..."

"Nah, I don't wanna hear shit. Just do as I say, beautiful. I got you." He silenced me with a kiss and opened the door for me to hop out the truck. "Put that money away. Aye, two hours should be enough, right?"

I tucked the money in my bra then thought about where I was. "I guess. Wait, hold up. What's wrong with the way my hair is now?" I frowned and touched my quick weave. I just knew I'd made my hair store bundles blend in perfectly, but now I wasn't so sure. A wave of insecurity came over me.

Snookie leaned out the window and interrupted what Dolph was about to say. "Uhh, nothing at all, Tahiry. Just, you know, go spice it up a little. Ya man got something real special planned for y'all." He winked at me.

I started cheesing and then jumped in Dolph arms. I placed a juicy kiss on his lips. "Okay then! I'mma make sure I look extra good for you."

He slapped me on my ass and replied, "Aight, I'll be back, beautiful. Go inside."

I watched as he hopped back inside the Bentley, blew me a kiss and Snookie screeched off. I stood on Newbury Street in front of *Dellaria's* and took a deep breath before walking inside. The salon was beautiful and comforting. I noticed for midday on a Saturday the salon was completely empty. I approached the receptionist and cleared my throat. "Umm, hi...I'm here to..."

"Welcome to Dellaria's! I'm Misty. Are you Tahiry?"

I chuckled nervously and shook her hand as she extended it for me to shake. "Yeah, but how did you-"

"Giiiirl! Your man is the shit girl! He rented out the whole salon and told us to get rid of every customer just for you. You lucky as hell!" This Spanish chick got amped as hell, hugging on me all excited and shit, then checked herself. "Oops, I forgot I was at work. Sorry. But seriously, you're one lucky girl. Is Dolph really your boyfriend?"

"Misty!"

We both turned and made eye contact with this tall white chick who walked over shaking her head. "Please excuse her, Tahiry. I'm Amanda. Have a seat and let us work our magic." She rushed me into a salon chair and took my hair out from the rubber band. "I'm thinking blonde highlights."

"Blonde?"

"Yes, girl. I'mma beast with the weave believe it or not." Amanda winked at me through the mirror.

Misty added, "And my fingers work wonders with the makeup, girl. Trust me. You're gonna walk out of here looking like a celebrity!"

I felt bum rushed with all this shit but also excited for a little makeover. The way Misty reacted and the ugly bitches from earlier had me wondering just exactly who Dolph really was. It was evident he was somebody popular in Boston that all the bitches knew about...except for me. That alone had me a little more curious than before. I cleared my throat and asked, "Umm, are y'all are sure about this? Because..."

"Girl, yes. Whatever Dolph got planned for y'all must be special," Misty responded with a head nod.

Amanda added, "You should definitely feel special. Embrace it."

I nodded my head at what they were saying and decided to go with the flow. Fuck it. Why not? I'd never had a beauty makeover before and if Dolph was a hood celebrity, I wanted to look the part to be on his arm for the day. I gave in.

I told them, "Okay fine. Make me into an overnight celebrity then."

***

"Voila!"

"Damn, girl, you was pretty before but now... shit, even I'd fuck with you."

For two hours, I'd let Amanda and Misty pluck, trim, dye,

curl, add foundation, highlight, and give me a full set and pedicure. I was exhausted but when Misty held that mirror up to my face, I barely recognized myself.

"Oh, my God!" I gasped in amazement.

I stood up from the salon chair and walked up to the full-length mirror to admire my new look. My once okay yet store bought weave had been replaced with long Malaysian bundles. I had blonde and burgundy highlights through my hair, my face was beat to perfection and the stiletto nails I was rocking made my hands look like that of a true celebrity. Even the white gel polish on my toes had me feeling good. I was in awe and pure shock and they could definitely tell.

"Y'all did the damn thing! Thank you."

Amanda and Misty slapped each other five. "I told you we were the shit." Misty smirked at me.

"It also helped that you're a natural beauty anyway, Tahiry. All we did was enhance your look. That'll be $1,275."

My mouth almost hit the floor until I remembered the money in my bra that Dolph gave me. I handed it over and then flipped my bundles over my shoulders.

"Yes, bihhh, slayyyy!" Misty started twerking.

"You're so unprofessional. I swear…" Amanda shook her head as she walked over to the receptionist desk to write up the receipt. "Lemme get a picture for our Instagram page."

I was a little overwhelmed with everything but still, my ass posed for the camera. Laughing, I said, "I can't believe this. I look and feel… so differently. Like… wow. Thank you."

"Nah, girl, thank ya man."

"So, is he really your boyfriend? You're dating Dolph?" Amanda probed once again.

Smiling and nodding my head, I replied, "Yeah, well, you know..."

The salon door opened and in stepped Dolph and Snookie. Dolph's mouth opened wide and I blushed immediately. He started singing, "There goes my baabbbyyy..." We all laughed.

Snookie stated, "Damn, Tahiry. I almost didn't recognize you, girl."

"Stop playing. That's my baby right there. Come here, girl." Dolph motioned for me to walk over to him then he spun me around and planted a kiss on my lips. "You look so fucking good. Marry me right now."

"What? You so crazy!" I playfully pushed him away when he kissed me again. I could smell the liquor on his breath and taste the weed.

"You have no idea, ma. Ayo, y'all did a good job. Here's a lil' something extra." He went into his jeans and pulled out two crisp $100 bills for them each to take.

I watched as Amanda and Misty drooled over this nigga, my nigga, and I simply turned his face towards mine for another kiss. This time I sucked on his lips passionately and he gripped my waist. I put on a little show and moaned against his lips before turning to face the ones responsible for my makeover. It's funny because until this very moment, I couldn't see the hate in their eyes. That shit was evident now. I grinned.

"Thanks so much again, ladies." Winking at them, I linked hands with Dolph while Rock held the door open for us to walk out of *Dellaria's* hand in hand. The three of us hopped in the truck and Snookie sped off down Newbury Street.

"You really look dope, Tahiry. Like, so fucking dope. I wanna eat you alive," Dolph whispered in my ear.

Snookie asked, "To the airport, bro?"

"Airport?" I quickly asked and looked at Dolph like he was crazy. Where the hell was he trying to go? "What's he talking about?"

"I got something planned." He cuffed me around my neck and whispered in my ear again. "You fucking with me or nah? Please say yes, beautiful. Lemme show you something different."

The nerves settled in my belly. He had me curious and nervous at the same damn time. "I guess so. Yeah, I mean..."

"Nah, is you fucking with me or nah? It's a yes or no question, baby." He looked me in the eye and I could tell he was dead serious wanting a straight answer. At that moment, I felt safe with him. He was really trying to make up for last night's first impression and I had to give credit where it was due.

I smiled and nodded my head. "Yes, I'm fucking with you. But..." I watched his face screw up. "I'm afraid to fly."

Dolph laughed a little bit. "Don't ever be scared. Not with me, aight?" He cupped my face and kissed my lips. "I told you I won't hurt you. You're good with me. I promise you that."

And just like that, I forgot about everything. Everything like common sense, checking in with my mother and even hitting Jalika up about chilling later. Nothing else mattered but this natural high I was on. Dolph's energy was different than these lame ass Boston niggas. His vibe was different. *He* was different. I loved that shit. As Snookie drove to Logan, Dolph and I cuddled up and tongued each other down. Before long, we arrived then hopped on this cute little private jet to head to Philly. It was just the two of us. I was stunned! Nobody had ever shown me shit like this. He ate my pussy once more and had me crying and wanting to climb the walls. I believed him when he told me that the possibilities were endless.

Three

We stepped off the jet and slid right into a black stretch limo that was bringing us to The Bellevue Hotel in Downtown Philly. I rolled down the window and peeked my head out. Even though it wasn't too far from home, I'd never been to Philly.

"Yeah, shits kinda lit. There's always some shit to do unlike back in the hood." As if reading my mind, Dolph cuddled me from behind and said, "I can't wait to take a walk with you around the city."

I closed my eyes and imagined us cuddled up on a horse ride throughout the city and my whole body started to tingle all over. He didn't even seem like the type, but he had me wanting to see what was up. All these years saving my virginity and here I was contemplating giving it to a nigga I'd only known for less than a day. Crazy shit. Dolph was definitely on a different level compared to list of the niggas that tried to breeze my way. Everything happened for a reason. He was interesting and had me interested to the fullest. I peered over my shoulder and smirked at him.

"Is that right?"

"Most definitely. You're fucking beautiful. I'm just glad you took this chance on a nigga. No bullshit, I'mma show you what type of time I'm on. You hear me?" He turned my face towards his. "I'm here to finally show you what real is."

"I hear you. And I bet you can hear my stomach too." I laughed and touched my growling belly. "I'm starving. You got me getting makeovers and catching flights and shit."

He laughed with me. "My fault, beautiful. We definitely gon' eat. What you in the mood for?"

"Ummm, maybe some steak and shrimp?" I licked my lips.

"My type of woman. Shit, you definitely ain't scared to eat. I like that shit." He grinned. The limo stopped rolling. The driver announced we had arrived at our destination and that there was a car waiting for us by valet. "Aight, man, good looks." Dolph tipped the driver a hundred, reached for the duffle bag on the floor by his feet and we both hopped out to walk inside the hotel.

"Damn! This shit looks like something straight out of a magazine." My basic ass couldn't keep my mouth closed. I was in awe. We linked arms and headed to check in.

"Good evening, Mr. Farrow. Welcome back. Here's your room keys and please let us know if you need anything." The front desk agent greeted us with a warm smile.

"Yeah, I actually need the clothes in this bag pressed and steamed to be ready in a like an hour, Destiny. Thanks." Dolph winked and handed her a hundred dollar tip along with the duffle bag.

"Anything for you, sir." The chick slipped the money into her bra and walked off from the service desk.

I instantly got a slight attitude and looked over at Dolph, who just gently pulled me towards the elevators. Once inside, I asked, "So lemme guess? You take all your hoes here for the weekend, huh?" I shook my head.

"Correction. I don't take hoes anywhere." He mean mugged me then his demeanor changed. "I, uh, actually have family out here and had a death in the family a few months back.

So a couple family members crashed here and I footed the high ass bill." I felt bad for assuming and lowered my head. Sighing, he lifted my head and said, "Stop assuming I'm one of the bad guys, aight? I'mma good nigga, Tahiry."

"I hope so."

"Come on." The elevator dinged to let us know we'd reached the top floor. "You're gonna love this suite. Trust me. The view is amazing."

I held his hand and we walked down to the presidential suite. Dolph slid the key in the door and I was immediately met with pink and red rose petals on the floor throughout the entire suite. There were big ass balloons that read "Hey Beautiful" and "Forgive Me". There was a big ass teddy bear holding a Victoria's Secret bag on the California king sized bed. My mouth hit the floor.

"Dolph..." My eyes watered and I choked back the tears. This nigga was something else already. How the hell did he pull this shit off? I was speechless as I stood in front of the bed and stared at him.

He smiled and hugged me tight then whispered in my ear, "I told you you're good with me. Last night wasn't a good first impression, so I hope this makes up for it."

I kissed and sucked on his neck. "It definitely does." We stared each other down for a second and something came over me that made me reach for the zipper on his jeans. I slipped my tongue in his mouth and we tongue wrestled for a second until Dolph pulled away from me.

"What's wrong?" I looked up at him, feeling horny as shit. I wanted him to take my virginity right then and there. I wanted to feel his big strong arms pull me closer to him as he fucked me silly. I wanted to feel my walls hug his dick closely. I wanted to feel his sweat dripping on my body. I wanted to feel everything that I knew I was missing out on.

Kissing my forehead, Dolph laughed and asked me, "Don't you wanna eat? I mean, you've been feeding me all day but some real food is definitely needed, beautiful."

I chuckled and slightly rolled my eyes. "Okay... let's eat. Where we going?"

"Anywhere you wanna go."

I hugged him around his neck and couldn't help but ask this burning question. "Why me? You coulda bagged any bitch last night and took any bitch outta the hood for the night. Why me? I'm struggling, I'm simple and basic as fuck and-"

"Stop that. Let's just say I see what I want and I go after it. You stood out from the rest." Dolph moved my hair out of my face and continued. "You're special. If you don't see that, I'll show you that shit. Understand me? I'mma show you something different. As long as you tell me you're fucking with me and you riding with me, I got you. I'm tryna fucks with you heavy, Ty."

I let out a sigh of relief. I felt confident that he was telling me the truth and not just trying his luck with me. He really went all out and I felt like he was genuinely speaking from the heart. It wasn't hard for me to see I would be falling hard for him in no time at all. In just a short amount of time, he had me doing shit I dreamed of and feeling ways I only imagined from reading hood books. Was this all a dream? The slap on my ass from Dolph made me realize this was indeed reality.

"I'll be right back, beautiful." He winked at me and left the room.

I wasted no time calling up Jalika. I had to tell her this shit, but who knew she would react the way she did. "Bitch, what the hell you mean you're in Philly? Philadelphia?! You don't even know that nigga! He's a shooter, Ty. What if he's some killer nigga and your ass ain't never coming back to Boston?"

"What? Girl, shut up. I didn't even know I was going until we were going, J! Damn. It just...kinda happened!" I said in a hushed voice into my phone.

I went into the huge bathroom where everything was made out of marble and sat on the edge of the tub. I turned the shower on and listened as Jalika cussed my ass out. I needed to tell her what was up with me and Dolph so she wouldn't go to my crib looking for me, which would make my mother suspicious. I needed her to think Jalika and I were together. So I told her ass to play along when I got back to Boston and of course she started rashing!

Jalika sucked her teeth. "Uh uh, you ain't even right, Tahiry. He must be some kind of special."

"He got me feeling like the special one, shit..." I smiled into the phone, feeling like a high school girl with a big ass crush on the baddest boy in school. "He's doing something to me already, J. I can't even describe it, but this shit feels so weird but good."

"Bitch, lemme find out you in love and shit! Ooooh!"

"Nah, nah. No love but... it's something. It's like I'm under a spell or some shit, J. I can't even describe this shit, but all I know is I'm riding this shit out 'til the wheels fall off."

"You got your hair done, nails and some more shit. Check you the fuck out! I'm jelly though." Jalika frowned and rolled her eyes.

"You know I'll bring you back something and I'mma see wassup with the white boy for you, okay? Bitch, I got you," I whispered into the phone. "Just when I get back, we gotta tell my mother we came out here together."

Shit, as many times I done covered for Jalika's ass during

high school, she owed me more than this favor. I was grown, I just didn't want my mother grilling me on Dolph. I'd never even mentioned the dudes I used to talk to before because my mother would have asked them to come over so she could pick their brains and shit. Dolph wasn't exactly Mr. Perfect being in the streets and I was almost certain the money he flaunted was drug money, so meeting my mother was a no go. At least not right now. I wanted to keep him a secret and all to myself.

"I got you, Ty. I want a fly ass outfit! Oh and some shoes too!"

I laughed. "I don't know about that, heffa, but I got you. I'll hit you in a few." I ended the call and got ready to shower. Of course, as soon as I started up my playlist, Kehlani's voice started singing to me so I sang along…*"I'm looking right at you, but you're not there. I'm seeing right past you, but you seem well aware. Your body is here but your mind is somewhere else so far gone and you think I can't tell. Can't tell that you are disconnected…you pulled away. And I miss your presence. I always said to you. Baby you should be here, right here. Baby you should be here, right here. Don't know where you went but you're lost now. Don't know where you went but you're gone now."*

I loved her song *You Should Be Here*. I was really in the shower piping it. I didn't even hear Dolph come into the bathroom until I heard, "Yo'! You can sing?" He paused the music and pulled the shower glass door back with a huge grin on his face.

Shyly, I replied, "I mean, yeah…I do a lil' something." I tried hiding my body from him as he stared me down with this look in his eyes.

"Nah, you can do more than that. And don't hide from me." He told me and slapped my ass. "You're beautiful and you can sing your ass off."

"Thank you."

He started to brush his teeth while I showered and I smiled to myself thinking this was just like a scene from a movie. I decided to see what was up with his friend and Jalika. "So, you know my friend wants to see what's up with the white boy you was with last night. I guess she's digging him."

"Oh yeah, she's feeling my nigga?" Dolph asked with his mouth full of toothpaste. "Aight. I'll see what's good with him when we get back to the hood. For now, let's get ready so I can feed you, beautiful."

We got dressed to head to The Capital Grille looking like money! I was wearing a spaghetti strap burgundy dress with a plunging neckline that had my titties sitting lovely. The gold Giuseppe's on my feet with the matching shoulder bag and diamond studs in my ear along with the matching bracelet had me feeling like royalty. I was surprised that after my bomb ass shower that my curls were still intact. After a little touch up, my face was still beat to the heavens. I'd never looked more flawless in my life and I had Dolph to thank for that. I rolled my old clothes up and tossed them shits inside of a plastic bag. I reached inside the fridge in the kitchenette area and pulled out the chilled bottle of Remy that was waiting. I needed a shot and I needed it now.

"Damn, you starting the party without me?"

"Well, I was..."

I turned around holding the bottle in my hand and my eyes traveled from Dolph's head down to his feet. *Goddamn, this nigga is fine as fuck.* He was dressed in a black suit with a handkerchief and Tom Ford loafers the same color as my dress. His dreads we pulled back neatly and his beard was trimmed to perfection. He flashed me a wide grin and I noticed he'd taken his grill out of his mouth. The watch on his wrist was shining just as much as the diamond stud in his ear. This nigga was the truth! I immediately threw back the bottle to take a big swig of the

Remy.

He laughed at me and said, "I guess you like how a nigga cleans up, huh?

"Hell yeah. Why you so damn fine, bruh?"

Walking over to me, Dolph took the bottle to guzzle then place it back in the fridge. "You the fine one, baby." He took my hand to twirl me around. "You ready to go?"

"I definitely am." I smiled up at him and we left the hotel.

During dinner, I decided to pick his brain. The way he had me feeling had to be illegal or I was plain, ol' bat shit crazy. Either that, or I was definitely under a spell. I just had to know more about him. The restaurant was upscale and fancy and the hostess sat us on the patio for a candlelit dinner all to ourselves.

"Dolph, you really did all this?" I asked him as he pushed my seat up to the table. "Just for...me?"

He took a seat across from me and flashed a grin. "Yes, just for you. I told you I see something in you these bitches don't have. I really wanna make you mine."

"Well, I gotta know more about you. For one..." I paused to take a sip of the red wine the waitress had poured for us. "Am I really safe with you? Last night was... crazy."

Dolph sighed and shrugged his shoulders. "Aight, I'm not gon' lie to you. I'mma popular nigga. I got drama with a few people, but I handle mine and I'll never put you in harm's way as I told you before. I didn't expect that shit to go down last night. I can't say I'm sorry enough." He reached for my hand. "All I can do is show you what it is."

"I hear you. I just don't want a repeat of that shit. You seem a lot smarter and better than that."

"I am. I'm tryna put this street shit on the back burner

one day once I got enough money saved up to eat off of," he explained, looking at me intently.

"I see. So what is it that you do exactly?" I questioned, although I already had a strong idea what he did for a living.

Dolph laughed a little bit and massaged his beard. "You ain't stupid, beautiful. You know what I do. I'mma hustla and I'm the best there is, feel me? Anything you want or need, I can provide you with." Blushing, I pushed my bang out of my face as I listened to him. He continued, "Nah, I'm dead serious. If you really fucking with a nigga, I got you. I keep telling you that. If you wanna sing, we can make shit happen. I don't even want you working in that funky ass department store no more actually."

"What? I mean, I need my little coins and shit. It's not much but-"

"It ain't shit," he told me, aggressively. "No offense. I'm just saying, I can put some real money in your pockets if you really wanna get paid." Just then, the waiter came over to take our order. Dolph ordered us both steak, shrimp and Cajun lobster with side Caesar salads. I couldn't wait to demolish my food. I waited until the waiter was out of earshot before asking what he meant buy his last statement.

"Some real money?" I raised an eyebrow at him as I sipped my wine. "What you mean by that?"

"I could always use a little assistant. Bagging up and shit. Doing a couple drop offs for me as well. Whatever your lil' job was paying you, I could double that a week. Plus, you my baby now, right? Whatever you want, you got it. So what's up?"

I sat back, eyeballing this nigga and really contemplating his offer. I wasn't a scary chick when it came to hustling. It actually intrigued me, but I just never came across the person to get down with. Was I really thinking about doing the shit he mentioned? Absolutely. I wanted to quit Macy's the day I got hired and low and behold, I finally could leave that annoying ass job. Could he really help me with this singing shit? I always dreamed of signing to a major label. But was this shit all too good to be true? I couldn't help but wonder. As I battled with my thoughts, Dolph interrupted me.

"Take your time to think about it, aight. Just don't make me wait too long, beautiful." He winked at me and I winked back. I could tell this was the start of something serious and I was praying it was the start of something good.

During dinner, we talked about everything from our childhoods to most recent shit. We were both December babies, but I was born in the beginning and him at the end. Dolph told me about how he grew up in the hood and his father put him on to hustling. It was all he knew and he informed me he was damn good at it. At twenty seven, eight years older than me, he was a millionaire. He mentioned that he was looking for a wife to settle down and really build a foundation with somebody. Dolph told me he just knew deep down that somebody was me. I told him about my upbringing with my struggling single mother, niggas I once talked to, my horrible ass job and my plans of being famous one day. He told me he knew some people in the music business and he could definitely help me out if I was going to take shit seriously.

After we wined and dined, we jumped in a taxi and then walked around Downtown just as he said we would. Dolph bought me an anklet that read "Beautiful" and big, gold, hoop earrings. He really made me feel special and like I was the only girl in the world on some Rihanna shit. The feeling was indescribable. I never once checked my phone either. Nothing else mattered but him and us at this moment. It was just us. As the night went on, I felt so comfortable with him like we'd known each other forever. I couldn't help but wonder if God himself sent this man to the House of Blues just for me. I had to stop questioning everything though. It just felt right.

We got back to the hotel around nine that night and my feet were killing me. Dolph ran me a bath and promised to rub me down when I got out. He was a man of his word. I got out of the tub and there was a silk nightie waiting on the bed for me. Old school R&B was playing low in the background and Dolph was waiting in the bed smoking a blunt of course. I smiled at him. He looked like a God. I was feeling like a goddess as I slipped into the nightie. I just knew we were going to fuck and I would no longer be a virgin. To my surprise, Dolph gave me a massage and told me he wanted to take his time with me. He told me I was worth waiting for. It was then I knew that he knew I was a virgin, but how? Even to this day, I didn't know he knew, but he did. I didn't feel ashamed though. We laid up watching movies and laughing like best friends until I fell asleep in his arms.

Four

"Where the hell are you at, Tahiry Monroe? And why haven't you been answering my calls or my texts? You got me losing my mind thinking something is wrong with you! Jalika's phone is going straight to voicemail too. I know y'all up to no good. You need to call me!"

"Shit!" I jumped up out the bed when I heard my phone ringing, but I missed the call. I checked my phone and saw I had eleven missed calls, seven text messages and two voicemails from Jalika and my mother. Listening to that voicemail from my mother made me sick to my stomach. Who the hell did I think I was disappearing with a nigga I barely knew? Granted I had a good time and dope night with Dolph, the reality of my real world came smacking me in the face.

"Fuck, fuck, fuck! Dolph, wake up." I shook him repeatedly. I had to get back to Boston before my mother flipped the fuck out.

"What's good, beautiful?" He mumbled in his sleep and rolled over, reaching for me. "You aight? Lay back down."

I shrugged him off and wiped my tears. "Nah, I'm not. I'm bugging. I don't even know you and here I am just leaving the hood all willy nilly." I rolled her eyes at him and pulled my hair back in a ponytail. "I gotta get back to Boston. My mother is tripping. I need to get my ass home." My chest was hurting from the anxiety I felt right now. I didn't care that I didn't look all put together anymore. I could feel my eyelashes hanging on for dear life after that bomb ass sleep on the plush pillows.

Dolph sat up and pulled me close to him. "Aight, aight. Relax. I mean, you grown, right?" He asked and held me by the shoulders to really look in my eyes. "You're nineteen, Ty. You ain't no little ass girl, right? Your mom's will be aight."

"No. You don't understand, dawg. My mother be on my back. I always check in. I don't pull disappearing acts, especially not with strangers." I sighed. "She'd kick my ass. I just need to get home. This was fun while it lasted." I tried to pull away from him, tried to get out of the bed, but he snatched back. Without warning, he kissed the shit out of me and suddenly, I felt my body loosen up.

Dolph broke the kiss away and told me, "Look, we gon' head back to the Bean and I'mma give you some money and a little gift for your mom's. Maybe she'll lighten up and be cool about you not coming home." I couldn't help but to raise an eyebrow at this nigga. He laughed. "What?"

I started shaking my head and said, "Dawg, I must be dreaming. You're too good to be true. Something is too good about you."

"I'mma good nigga, beautiful." I grinned. "Just tell me you fucking with me and everything will be good." I smiled up at him and sighed. "Go take a shower and fix your face. Eyelashes all fucked up and shit," He joked.

I playfully hit him in the chest. "Shut up." I went into the bathroom to fix myself and get ready to head back to Boston and back to reality. I was hoping and praying this feeling wouldn't go away and neither would Dolph. I turned the shower on and decided it was best to call my mother back before she sent a damn search team looking for me. I braced myself for the conversation and of course, it started off fucked up.

"Tahiry, where the hell are you? Are you alright? You

must be out your rabbit ass mind!"

"Ma, I'm fine. I'm sorry I didn't call you. Umm, me and Jalika hit on a scratch ticket and we hopped on the bus to Philly for the night. It was like spur of the moment. I bought you something nice too." I thought of a lie right on the fly. I was praying she bought the shit.

"Oh, so that means you don't know how to return a damn phone call or text in almost twenty four hours? I've been calling her phone too!" My mother scolded me. "That shit ain't cool, Tahiry. As much bull shit happening in this world and girls going missing all the damn time and you wanna pull a disappearing act! Have you lost your goddamn mind?"

"Ma, you do realize I am nineteen now, right? I mean, geesh. I think I can look out for myself. I'm not dumb!" I rolled my eyes, feeling like a little ass girl in trouble or some shit.

"Tuh, well as long as you live under my damn roof, you'll respect what I have to say and abide by what I mean! You need to inform me when you ain't gonna be coming home and at least giving me a heads up to where you're gonna be. Hello! Anything could go wrong! Do you understand me?"

"You treat me like such a child!" I shouted into the phone, no longer caring if Dolph could hear me on the phone or not. "I mean, damn! I've done everything right. I did well in school, I help around the house, and I got a job. I'm not pregnant or on drugs. I just wanna live my fucking life!" I went the hell off on my mother.

"Excuse me? You *are* a damn child. You may be turning twenty in three months but you don't know shit from piss. You barely have a decent job and you're not ready to even be on your own!" My mother sighed. "Look, when you get home, we have to talk because this cannot happen again if you plan on living here, Tahiry. I mean that shit. I was worried to death."

Dolph walked in the bathroom and leaned up against the doorframe, looking at me with a concerned look on his face. I sucked my teeth and turned my back to him and replied, "Ma, I'll just talk to you later." I didn't bother waiting for her response before I ended the call and turned my phone on *Do Not Disturb.*

"Yo', you good?" Dolph walked over and hugged me from behind. "Talk to me."

Sighing, I told him, "I'm good. Lemme get ready real quick and we can go." I quickly showered and got dressed in my clothes. My hair was still bouncy as shit, but I decided to rock it in a tight bun so my mother wouldn't notice too much of a difference. I'd even fixed my eye lashes too. Looking in the mirror, I felt regular again and I wasn't feeling it, but it was whatever for the moment. I just had to get my ass back home.

When we got back to Boston, of course Snookie was waiting at the airport in the red Bentley with the music blasting, smoking a blunt. Dolph and I climbed in the backseat and hugged up. I couldn't believe how I fell for him overnight. He had me under a spell that I never wanted to break free from. Snookie passed him the blunt and Dolph told him to head towards the South End before they started shooting the shit.

Hold up... I immediately butted into their conversation. "Dolph, you know that I gotta get home. My mother-"

"Relax, beautiful. I got you." He brought my hand up to his lips for a kiss. "I just gotta make a couple of stops before I bring you home. Aight?"

"I don't know. I feel like I need to get home now." I was shitting bricks because my mother was still flipping out. I would never hear the end of this shit.

"We gon' stop by the bank and open up an account for you, then I'mma give you some money for your mom's, aight?"

My mouth fell open. Did I just hear this nigga correctly? Nah, I was tripping. "I'm sorry… what?"

"You heard me. Buy some clothes, shoes, jewelry and whatever you want or anything you need. I'm sure your mom's could use extra bread, right? I really don't want you working at fucking Macy's, Tahiry."

"Wait a minute." I placed my hands on his chest and squinted my eyes at him. "You're serious? Why? Why are you doing all of this?"

"Don't ask why. Just be grateful you got a nigga like me in ya life." He kissed my lips and with a smile said, "Now sit back and enjoy the ride."

When we actually pulled up to Chase bank on Washington Street, I started cheesing like a muthafucka because Dolph was dead serious about this shit. I couldn't stop thinking about all the new shit I was about to buy for myself and of course, I would grab Jalika things too. And then there was my mother, who I was so nervous to introduce to Dolph, but I was kind of anxious as well. I couldn't wait to see her face when she saw how he was coming through for her. I wouldn't have to waste my time at stupid ass Macy's anymore just to give away my little bit of money. I saw my struggle days ending… just like that.

Dolph opened up a bank account and I was issued a temporary debit card that day with a balance of five thousand dollars. He told me that was just the start of things. Before we left the bank, he handed me a check for ten racks and a bitch almost passed the fuck out. He said it was for my mother and to secretly pay off the rent and bills for the rest of the year first thing Monday morning. We left the bank holding hands, but he wasn't done yet. When we hopped back in the truck, we drove Downtown and Dolph went into E.B Horn's, the jewelry shop. He came back out in under ten minutes, jumped back in the truck and handed me a jewelry box. Inside were a pair of diamond and pearl chandelier earrings to die for. He told me they were for my mother as a gift and I just knew she wouldn't be too mad about me staying out all day and night. Fuck a cloud nine, I was chilling with the stars feeling a way I never had before. Cherished. Wanted. Appreciated. I was feeling like a queen. Now all I had to do was meet with Jalika to get this story straight.

"Damn, a nigga feel like he driving Miss Daisy," Snookie complained. "Can we get back to the fucking money or nah? Shit."

"Shut up!" We both shouted.

"We 'bouta wrap this shit up now, nigga." Dolph reached under the seat and whipped out a bottle of Remy. He took a huge swing then motioned for me to take one.

I chuckled. "What? It's too early," I declined.

"Scaredy cat." He mocked me and started to put the bottle back under the seat.

I twitched my lips to the side thinking what the hell. It may only have been noon in Boston, but it was five o'clock somewhere in the world. "Hmmm, on second thought, gimme that." I took the bottle and tipped it up. I shook off the warm, strong taste. I could feel the burn traveling through my body. Dolph smirked at me just as his phone rang. It blasted through the speakers in the truck.

"Yo' bro, that's Big Mama," Snookie told him, looking back with a look I couldn't describe plastered on his face.

We stayed cuddled up as Dolph rubbed his beard and replied, "Pick it up." He kissed my cheek. "It's just my grandmother, beautiful. What's up, Big Mama? Everything good?"

"Yeah, boy, I'm good over here. I was just checking on you. Hello Snookie." I heard his grandmother sigh into the phone. "You know who has been by here looking for you, Dolph."

Dolph spoke. "I'm heading back to the hood now. I'll talk to you about that in a few." He cleared his throat and shifted a little bit like he wanted some space, so I backed up off him.

"You need to face that reality, son. I'm telling you..."

Dolph cut her off aggressively. "Listen, I'mma figure some shit out, Big Mama. I gotta go."

"Randolph..."

"I'll stop by in a few."

Snookie ended the call on the Bluetooth and shook his head. "You know she's right, bro."

Dolph banged on the headrest, damn near hitting Snookie in the head. "Nigga, did I fucking ask you? Why the fuck you speaking on this shit anyway?"

"I'm just saying-"

BAM! A car slammed right into the back of the Bentley.

"What the fuck?" We all wondered aloud.

Snookie slammed on the breaks and looked up in the rear-view mirror, then Dolph immediately reached under the seat and pulled a gun out. My face screwed up wondering what the fuck was going on then. Dolph kind of relaxed a little bit but got annoyed at the same time.

"Dawg, what the fuck?" He said.

"Dolph..."

"Bro, I know that's not who I think it is..." Snookie mumbled, shaking his head.

"Stay in the truck, aight, beautiful?"

"What the fuck is going on, Dolph?" I asked just before he and Snookie jumped out of the truck in the middle of a green light. Cars started beeping and swerving around both cars. "Go the fuck around! Man, I should have known her ghetto ass would be showing up sooner than later. That's probably why she was blowing my phone up all fucking day!" I heard Dolph yell and I immediately looked out the tinted back window to see what the fuck was up.

I saw this bony ass, light skin chick with fucked up clothes getting out of a beat-up Camry. The bright red wig she wore was pulled up in a messy ass bun like it hadn't been brushed in days. Who the fuck was this bitch? My eyes and ears were glued to the scene.

"I should fuck your dumb ass up!" Dolph shouted at her and pointed his finger as she ran up on him.

"Britney, get back in the car!" A girl shouted out the window of the Camry.

"Nisha, mind your business right now, bitch!" The Britney girl snapped then shoved Dolph in the chest. "I know it was you who got me kicked out of my shelter, Dolph! Where the fuck am I supposed to go now? Huh? How could you do me like this?! You said you loved me!"

"Love? Bitch, look at you!" He laughed in her face. "If you wanna be around here looking like you on that shit, that's your fucking business, but you ain't gon' be my bitch." Dolph shook his head my head and frowned at her with disgust. "I told you what to do." *So this was his ex, huh? Ugh, what the fuck was he thinking? She looks smoked the fuck out!* I thought to myself as I continued to be nosy, not missing a beat. "I'm good. Get the fuck away from me, Britney." He shoved her backwards and turned to walk towards the passenger side of the truck, shaking his head.

"Just go home, Brit," Snookie told her, looking like he felt sorry for the bitch.

"Leave me the fuck alone, Snookie! Yo', on God, fuck you,

Randolph!" Britney started to attack him from behind crying hysterically. "This is all your fault anyway. I swear to God, I fucking hate you! I wish I never fucking met you! You did this to me, muthafucka!"

"Did what?" Dolph towered over her with a look that put the fear of God in Britney's heart. It was written all over her face. I swallowed hard as I watched everything. "Watch what the fuck you say, Britney."

"I ain't watching shit."

Snookie jumped in between them and said, "Yo', bro, fuck her. Let's go nigga!"

"Shut up, Snookie! You ain't shit but his fucking errand boy. Bitch!" Britney spazzed, sniffling and some more shit. She tried to smooth down her wrinkled clothes and fucked up hair. "Just give me some money for a hotel or something. My car's all fucked up. I'm fucked up. Please, Dolph. I'm begging you!"

"Go about ya business, Britney. For real. You had a chance to ride this wave and you couldn't handle it. Be gone." He gave her a final look and stared directly at her until she got the hint. She sucked her teeth and balanced her weight from one side to the other, probably thinking if she should test his gangsta or not.

"Hmm, you probably got a bitch in the back of that ugly ass truck, huh? I bet the bitch can hear me. If so, run, bitch! Run! He ain't shit! He's-"

"Get the fuck in your car, Britney!" Snookie yelled at her and dragged her away from Dolph as he walked over to the truck. I quickly jumped back to where I was sitting and tried to look like I wasn't being nosy.

Dolph slid back inside and sighed while looking at me. "I'm sorry about that, Tahiry."

"Everything good?"

"I'm always good." He smiled at me. "That was my crazy ass ex. She's coked up and probably off her meds. I'm sorry you had to see that."

"That shit seems fresh still." I gave him the side eye of confusion. "What happened with y'all?"

"That's the past." Dolph reached for my hand to kiss. "You the future. Don't even worry about that, but I'm sorry you had to hear me get outta character." He caressed my cheek and tiled my chin up so we were eye to eye. "You forgive me?" He kissed my lips gently. Snookie hopped back in the truck and peeled off.

"Y'all niggas is fucking crazy..."

I hesitated on answering him because I really thought his interaction with the girl was weird. I never responded and we were all silent for about ten minutes before, out of nowhere, Dolph said, "Yo', Snookie, stop the fucking car, bro." His voice changed and the look in his eyes made him look deranged. My heart started pounding as I watched him reached under the seat again. Only this time, instead of pulling out the Remy bottle, it was a gun. He didn't even say shit to me as he tucked it in the back of his jeans.

"What now, nigga?" Snookie looked at me and then at Dolph, confused as fuck.

"Yo', you're scaring the shit outta me, Dolph. Can you just take me home now?"

Dolph ignored me and spoke to Snookie. "Pull around in the back of that crib right here and keep the car running," he told him. "I'll be right back," he snarled and gritted his teeth.

I gasped and covered my mouth when I saw Dolph damn near crack this old nigga's skull open in broad daylight in front of his door in Mission Hill. Who the fuck was this nigga I was

TASHA MARIE

falling for?

Five

"Snookie, do something! What the fuck?"

"Chill, Tahiry. You don't wanna fuck with him when he's in this kind of mood. Don't worry though." He gave me a light smile and said, "Everything's gon' be aight. Just chill."

Just chill? Dolph started beating the breaks off the old man who was probably around fifty years old or so. He didn't give a fuck. I heard him yell, "NIGGA, WHO THE FUCK GAVE YOU THE FUCKING CONFIDENCE TO PLAY WITH MY MUTHAFUCKING MONEY?" Wham! "DON'T YOU KNOW I WILL KILL YOUR BITCH ASS RIGHT HERE IN FRONT OF YA FUCKING CRIB?" Wham! "FUCKING FIEND! YOU READY TO LOSE YOUR LIFE OVER THIS SHIT?"

The old man pleaded. "Please, Dolph! Don't kill me, man! Please! I'll get your money, I'll get it!! I promise you, man. Just please don't kill me! Come on, Dolph, it's me..."

As I watched in horror with my eyes wide open and my heart pounding, it was evident that Dolph wasn't hearing shit this old ass nigga was saying. A woman swung open the front door and yelled, "Willie, baby? Oh, my Heavens! What's going on?" I assumed she was the old man's wife.

Dolph continued to stomp him and beat his ass. Folks started coming out of their apartments, but it was like once they say what was happening, they went back inside to mind their business. It was mind blowing. I just knew the police right next door would be coming to lock Dolph's ass up for sure. I couldn't believe what the fuck I was watching. It took every-thing in me to not try to stop this shit. I felt bad as fuck and scared as hell all in the same.

"I don't give a fuck what you talking about, Willis!" Dolph shouted. "You already know how I get down, muthafucka! I let you hold some work and you thought that shit was gon' be free forever? Fucking fiend! You been ducking me for a minute, now where's my muthafucking money, old man?"

His wife cried out, "Oh Heavens, please stop this! Please!"

"Charlotte, baby..." Willis managed to mumble to his wife. "Just go... back...in the room."

"Willie..."

Dolph aimed his gun at the doorway and barked, "Bitch, can't you hear?" The wife ran back inside the house and slammed the door.

Snookie just sat in the front seat rolling up, bumping some music by *Duffle Bag Trappy* while I sat in the back seat, damn near about to cry for this old man. I couldn't take it any-more. I hopped out of the Bentley and ran over to him. Pulling his arm, I yelled, "DOLPH!!!" It was like I broke him out of a trance or some shit the way he looked at me. His eyes softened for a second and then he turned around and bashed Willis in his face, blood spewing everywhere.

Bending down, he whispered to the old man, "The next time you even think about hitting my phone, glancing my way or any fucking thing, I swear to whatever God you fucking pray to that I'll kill you. Do we have a muthafucking understanding, Willis?" Barely able to speak or move, the old nigga just nod-ded his head. Standing up, he tucked his gun away and wiped the sweat that dripped from my forehead. Then he snatched me up by the arm, dragging me back to the truck. "Didn't I tell you to stay in the fucking truck, Tahiry?" He shoved me inside and climbed in behind me. Snookie passed him a blunt to spark and then peeled out of the projects like nothing ever happened. "Next time, please do as I tell you, beautiful. Please," Dolph spoke calmly as he looked over at me. He was covered in the man's blood.

I was shaking like loose booty meat. "Are you fucking crazy, Dolph? That old ass man could die! Yo', take me the fuck home right now!" I pulled out my phone to call up Jalika. Dolph took my phone from me. "Gimme my phone." I choked back the tears that threatened to fall from my eyes. *This nigga was crazy as fuck! How would he be so gentle yet a monster at the same damn time?* I wondered.

"Bro, you finally caught up to that nigga. Word. Ain't no taking shorts over on this side. Fuck that." Snookie nodded his head and continued to drive pass Roxbury Community College.

"Who you tryna call?" Dolph asked me, holding onto my phone.

"Jalika. I need my phone, Dolph, or I'll jump outta this bitch while it's moving." We locked eyes and his left eye twitched a little bit before he tossed my phone on my lap. "Thank you." I scooted far the fuck away from him and held the phone up to my ear. "J, where you at?"

"Leaving Jeremy's crib. You mother's been calling me, Ty. You back yet?"

"Yeah. Meet me at Walgreens off Morton." I watched as Dolph cleaned his hands with some wipes and peeled his bloody, dirty Polo off then reach into a duffle bag for another crisp shirt.

"Aight, boo. I'm heading there now. You good though?" Jalika asked me.

I just looked over at Dolph who was staring at me. He didn't look mad, but I couldn't place the look on his face either.

63

It was weird. Focusing back on the phone conversation, I told Jalika, "I'll see you in a few." I ended the call and just stared out the window, clutching my tote bag close to me.

I still couldn't get over this shit. Maybe that ex of his was right when she told me to run. Dolph was dangerous as fuck. But when he moved closer to me to invade my personal space, I closed my eyes, loving the scent of him. It was invigorating. It made me weak for him. I couldn't explain how or why. I knew what he'd just done was wrong on so many levels yet and still, here I was laying on my back, letting him feast on my pussy again. Snookie closed the shutters once more. Dolph's tongue was addictive. The way my pussy reacted to him was mind blowing. The way he gripped my waist when I tried to push his head away as he attacked my clit was everything. The way he nibbled on the inside of my thighs had me stuck. It was like a game of cat and mouse. Dolph had indeed caught me. I rained all over his tongue and his beard then he kissed his way up to my lips.

Kissing me over and over and over again, he apologized. "I'm so sorry you had to see that. I'm so sorry, beautiful. Don't run away from me. I'm sorry, baby."

"You coulda killed that man. I mean, if I didn't stop you..." I shook my head, trying to shake the images from my memory.

"Let's not even talk about it, aight?" He kissed my lips again, this time sucking on my lips. I quivered. "We good?" I stared him in the eyes for a moment then he flashed that epic smile of his and said, "Please, beautiful."

Sighing, I decided to push the incident in the back of my head. Pointing my finger at him, I told Dolph, "You gotta promise that shit won't happen again. Ever."

"I promise, Tahiry. You'll never see that side of me again." He wiped his goatee off while I adjusted my leggings and fixed my hair.

I heard Snookie though the shutters jokingly say, "Y'all muthafuckas needa goddamn room. Shit!"

I giggled and blushed a little bit while Dolph finally sparked up the blunt and took a big pull from the shit. I was curious to know what it felt like to smoke. I just knew the shit gave Jalika's ass the munchies something fierce! I nodded my head and said, "Lemme hit that."

Dolph laughed, choking on the weed smoke. "What? Cut the shit."

"I'm serious. Just one pull. I wanna try it," I whined and pouted my lips at him.

"Sorry, beautiful." He winked at me.

I stuck my tongue out and replied, "Whatever."

I got dropped off at Walgreens and noticed Jalika waiting outside, talking to some nigga of course. Dolph told me to make sure I gave my mother the check and earrings and to call him later. I promised I would. He tongued me down and I hopped out of the Bentley. I hollered at Snookie and walked over to my best friend.

She hugged me like she hadn't seen me in years. "Finally, bitch! I was getting worried. Your phone is going straight to voicemail. What's up with that?"

"Shit!" I'd forgotten I put the shit on *Do Not Disturb* before leaving Philly. Checking my phone, I saw my mother was still going off, telling me to get my ass home. Fuck! "Girl, so here's the plan." I linked arms with Jalika as we started to walk towards my crib. "We both hit on a scratch ticket and went to Philly just because and that's where we came up on some dough at the casino. Aight?"

"Yeah, Ty, that's cool and all, but bitch, did you actually

bring me back something?" Jalika laughed.

Chuckling, I replied, "Yes, I got you some dope ass gold earrings. They're fly as hell." I pulled them out of my bag.

"Ooooh, these shits is nice!" She started grinning all hard as she quickly popped out her hoops and replaced them with the new ones. "You know I love me some hoops, bitch. Anyway, so, uh...you liking this nigga, huh? Clearly, you didn't hit at a casino so tell me what's really good." We made eye contact.

I sighed. "Well, he's a drug dealer, J, like the kind in them hood books we be reading. The nigga got bank! He said he don't want me working anymore and he'll take care of me and shit." I shrugged. "I'm feeling the fuck outta him."

"I hear you and that's all fine and dandy, but so quickly he wanna do all of that for you? Y'all don't even know each other, Ty. I'm saying-"

"Well, haven't you ever heard of love at first sight, bitch? Damn."

"Girl, bye! You love the money and attention." Jalika laughed and playfully pushed me. "Lie to yourself, not to me, best friend. Just be careful. Everything that glitters ain't really gold."

I frowned at her. "What you mean? You think he's playing me? I got a check and a bank account just for me that says he's dead serious." I popped my lips at her.

"That's good shit. For real, Ty. I'm not hating or nothing, trust me. I'm not," Jalika told me. "Just be careful. That's all. You're a sweetheart and Dolph is definitely older and more mature than you."

"I know." I grinned. "But I'mma lock that thang down!" We both laughed.

"Did y'all fuck, Tahiry?"

"What? Bitch, no!" I looked at her like she was crazy.

She didn't need to know he was eating my pussy like there was no tomorrow, nor did she need to know I planned on giving it up to Dolph the next time I got with him. How could I not? After how he just blessed me, I had to bless him back.

"Nah, but I do hear you, J. Thanks for looking out. I'm hoping for the best though. He really got me feeling some type of way already." We finally reached my front steps and before I could even turn the key fully in the keyhole, the door flew open.

"About goddamn time! Both of y'all get your asses in here!" My mother walked towards the living room and we followed.

"Remember the story, heffa," I whispered and pinched Jalika.

"Sit down!" We both sat down on the couch and looked up at my mother, waiting for her to continue, but she didn't say shit else besides, "Well? I'm listening."

"I'm sorry, Ma. Like I said, we-"

"Yeah, I know. You went to Philly! Why was it so hard to pick up a damn phone, Tahiry? Jalika? Huh? Don't y'all know this world is getting crazier and scarier by the day!"

"Well, my phone was actually dead most of the time, Ms. Monroe. So between the both of us using Ty's, hers kept dying as well. But guess what?"

"What, Jalika?" My mother rolled her eyes and folded her arms across her chest, ready to knock us out.

"We got you some things. Right, Ty?" Jalika gave me a look.

"Oh, right." I opened my bag to pull out the jewelry box and I also handed her the envelop with the check inside. "We won big at the casino and you know, Jalika knows about the rent and stacked bills, so we put our winnings together and got this check written out to you."

"Say what?" My mother snatched the envelope and ripped it open with the quickness. Her whole attitude and demeanor changed. Her mouth hit the floor and the tears formed in her eyes. "Oh, my God. Girls... You didn't have to do this. Oh, my God. Ten grand! Shit, I need to go to the casino with y'all." She stared at the check in disbelief.

I got up to hug my mother. "I'm sorry for not calling and cursing on the phone, Ma. I just wanted this to be a surprise. Coming home, the bus broke down on the highway and then my phone died when we got to South Station. I was safe and sound though. No worries." I kissed her cheek and smiled. "I got you, Ma."

"Yeah, Ms. Monroe. We're big girls now. We got this!" Jalika reassured her with a hug also.

"I'm speechless, girls." My mother smiled and then opened the jewelry box. "Just my type of earrings. Thank you." She kissed my forehead and hugged Jalika again. "I greatly appreciate this. You have no idea." She wiped the tears rolling down her cheeks. "Next time, though, please just answer the damn phone!"

Jalika and I laughed and replied, "Yes, ma'am."

"I'm gonna deposit this and pay down some of this debt first thing in the morning!" My mother jumped for joy. "Hallelujah! Whoo! I feel good!" We watched her electric slide her way on out the living room in pure happiness, no longer mad about my whereabouts. It was that easy. Jalika and I smirked at each other.

"Bitch, you might have hit a goldmine with this nigga. Ten racks? Damn!"

"See," I nodded my head. "I told you. He's the one." I felt

my life changing, just as Dolph said it would. I had him to thank for everything.

Six

PRESENT DAY

I sure did have Dolph to thank for everything, including a concussion, a black eye and hella cuts and bruises that would take forever to heal. I laid in the hospital bed all loopy from the drugs and mad at the world. I should have been dead and I just knew I was out there on that pavement from the car accident. I thought the shit was finally over but nope, here was God saving my ass again and the babies too. Fucking twins.

I'd been stressing bad lately walking on eggshells with this nigga that I didn't think nothing of it when my period went missing. Three weeks ago, on the late night while Dolph was passed out drunk, I took a home pregnancy test. That shit came back positive and I was keeping it to myself because I honestly just didn't know what to do. I didn't know what to do about a lot of shit but something had to give. Every fucking day I felt like I was losing more of myself and my sanity. I didn't recognize shit about me these days and it was scary. I'm not just speaking on my looks although I was pretty fucked up right now. My face was bruised and cut the fuck up and my right eye was black and blue. I cried and cried. As sad as it was to think about, this wasn't the first time I wished I was dead.

I attempted to kill myself two times trying to escape Dolph's ass. The first time I took hella sleeping pills and fell asleep in the bathtub. He came home to find me, stuck his fingers down my throat and used Naloxone to bring me back to life. The second time I tried to off myself, I jumped out of the Bentley on the highway and literally ran right in the middle of midday traffic screaming my head off. I prayed a car would hit me and take me out but it didn't happen. Dolph dragged me back to the car while Snookie threatened some white couple who hopped out of their minivan. Man, Dolph beat the shit out of me in the backseat for "pulling another stunt". Needless to say, we didn't make it to the mall that day. Shaking my head, I just couldn't understand why God was keeping me alive. I just wanted to be free.

Well, I guess somebody cared about my ass the other day because they called the ambulance and I was rushed to Mass General Hospital. I was told I started bugging out in the hospital when I finally came to realization that I wasn't dead. I don't remember that shit but the doctors had to sedate me and I was restrained to the bed in an attempt to calm me down. Police showed up asking about the hit and run to which they had no leads. This real nice nurse, Laura, kept checking on me more than usual while I was in the hospital. I appreciated her but inside, I was feeling so fucked up. There was no telling how much more bullshit I could take.

The door to my room opened up and I quickly wiped my face. Clearing my throat, I said, "Hey, Nurse Laura. I was wondering when..." My words trailed off when I noticed it wasn't my usual nurse coming to check on me, but a tall ass, fine black man holding a huge bouquet of flowers and a teddy bear. He was as chocolate as my favorite Hershey's bar and over six feet tall with broad shoulders and bowlegged. Dressed down in a plain white tee, gray sweats and Nikes on his feet, rocking a Philly fitted hat, I wondered who the hell he was and if Dolph sent him. In his nose was a tiny stud, which looked good on him. His lips were full and caught my attention when he smiled at me.

"Tahiry?"

"Umm...maybe." He smiled at me and walked over to place the flowers next to my bedside. I kept my eyes on him the whole time. He handed me the fluffy teddy bear. "Thank you.

Who are you?"

He tapped his head and said, "That's right. You were kinda out of it when I first stopped by. My fault, love. I'm Gotti." He extended his hand and I lowered my head in embarrassment. I knew my face looked as fucked up as it felt.

"Well, Gotti... what do you want?"

He chuckled. "I just wanted to see you." I glanced his way when he took a seat in the chair next to my bed and licked his lips with a serious look on his face. "In case you didn't know, I'm the one who found you in the intersection and called the ambulance for you. I waited here until they told me you were gon' live. Real shit, I'm just here to check on you. You know, make sure you're alright and shit."

I was speechless. Who was this fine ass man to be caring about me? I wasn't shit but damaged goods but I did feel like I owed him a response. I simply nodded my head and toyed with the teddy bear as I replied, "Thank you for...what you did. You shoulda left me there though. You really should have." I shook my head.

"What? Why would you say some shit like that? Shit, if it were me..."

"But it wasn't you!" I lashed out and looked up at him. "It was me. Stupid ass me! Now here I am, alive and gotta go back to..." I stopped myself from saying anything else. He didn't need to know my current life events and what I was trying to escape from. He didn't need to know shit about me. "Look, I appreciate your help and all, but you can leave now. You shouldn't be here." I rolled my eyes and sucked my teeth, trying to hold back to tears that were going to fall down any minute now.

Gotti stood up and pinched the bridge of his nose. He sighed and said, "Hey. Look at me for a second." I bit the inside of my cheek, not really wanting to look at this man again, but I did anyway. He leaned down and said, "I know all them bruises on you ain't just come from this bad ass accident. You can lie to them doctors all you want to, but I've seen shit like this before. My sister used to let a nigga abuse her until she smartened up." I started to say something but he held his hand up. "No need to say anything right now, but on some real shit, I'm here for you. If you need to talk or whatever, I'm here." He softly caressed my cheek and I shyed away. I didn't know how to feel about it or anything that he just said to me. "I'll leave my number with the cool nurse who's been with you, aight?" He winked at me and walked out of the room.

For a moment, I sat there staring at the door feeling weird as hell. For the past year and a half, I'd been hiding the fact that Dolph hit me and here was this complete stranger that didn't know me from a whole in the wall, able to see what was really up with me. It broke my heart that my own mother was oblivious to everything. She either knew and didn't care or she really had no fucking clue what her daughter was going through. She was too caught up enjoying the perks of me fucking with Dolph, including her new luxury apartment, car, clothes and some more shit. The only time we spoke is when she wasn't shopping or taking a trip somewhere. It was sad to think I used to be that way in the beginning with Dolph; shut off from the world and only into myself and what I wanted to do. That muthafucka bought us and my mother had changed so much, I knew my secrets weren't of any interest to her ass.

Snookie was too much of a bitch boy to do something about it and Kase didn't really care for me since day one. And then there was Big Mama, who I figured was too old to see what was happening to me. I just knew it would tear her world apart to know her grandson was a monster in flashy ass clothing. A real devil in disguise. Dolph had everybody fooled or hypnotized and I wanted to break free of the bullshit and his spell. I wanted out. Although I was just rude as hell to him, I couldn't front. I was grateful for this Gotti person. He gave me another chance.

"Well, well, well…" My eyes shot up and landed right on Dolph's happy ass face. I was thinking, the nerve of this arrogant ass nigga to come waltzing up in this bitch a whole day and a half later! I swear, I couldn't stand him. As he walked over to the bed holding my purple Northface and a small duffle bag, it was so hard to believe how much I hated this man when I used to sweat the hell out of him. "It's nice to see you alive and well, beautiful. I brought you some clothes and a jacket." He smiled, dropped the bag to the floor and put the coat on the chair. He leaned down to kiss me and I quickly turned my head.

"Thanks, I guess, but I've been here since yesterday morning and you're just coming to see if I'm alive? Which hoe kept you busy, Dolph? Leah or Mnay?"

"See, this is why you be getting smacked," he snarled at me and sat on the edge of the bed. "You always got some slick shit to say, man. No cap, I'm really happy you aight." Yeah, because I believed that shit. How a strange ass nigga have the decency to bring me gifts and my so-called boyfriend didn't come with shit but his fucking bad energy?

The room grew awkwardly silent as we just stared at each other. I'd noticed the cut on his forehead was nothing compared to my bruises and shit. This situation was getting out of control. I frowned at Dolph and squinted my eyes at him then said, "I know you had something to do with that black truck slamming into my shit. I know you did. You ain't shit, Dolph."

He looked at me like I had eight heads before laughing like I'd just told the biggest fucking joke of all time. "You crazy, you know that?" He asked then looked at his watch. "Look, I-"

"You're the fucking crazy one!" I shouted. "Why can't you just do right by me or leave me the fuck alone? Why? Why do you keep doing this to me? This is not how shit was supposed to be. You promised!"

"I *can* do right by you and I be trying! Fuck you mean? I can't help it if you piss a nigga off sometimes, Ty."

"You ain't gotta hit me, Dolph. You stay fucking other bitches. I'm ugly, right? I'mma bum bitch, right? You tell me that all the time and you treat me like shit! Why pick me up just to beat me down? I coulda stayed doing what the fuck I was doing when you met me!" I rolled my eyes and folded my arms across my chest. I was so mad. I was hoping somebody heard us arguing and came to my rescue.

Dolph gripped my ankle and I winced in pain, giving him the death stare. "Fix your fucking face and stop all that yelling before I slap the fuck outta you up in this muthafucking hospital, Tahiry. Don't get cute. Fuck 12, and you know I don't give a flying fuck about no bitch ass security guard." He released the tight hold on my ankle and checked his phone.

Shaking my head, I told him, "It's always violence with you. What did I do to you? Huh? What the fuck did I do to make you hurt me over and over again? The fuck... I can't even get up to look in the mirror to see my face but trust me, I don't even want to."

"Aww, man, them lil' bruises will heal and you'll be back to sucking daddy's dick in no time, beautiful."

Rolling my good eye, I replied, "Dawg, I'm more than sure there's a bitch in your phone just for that. Why can't you just go be with somebody else and let me do me?"

I wasn't stupid. I knew for a fact that he was fucking around on me but honestly, I didn't care. The sexual chemistry between us faded a while ago and I hated sucking this nigga's dick after this one time I got a cold sore that took damn near two months to heal. Yet and still, he forced me to suck his dick most times. I barely got turned on by him for numerous reasons and the only time we fucked was when he came home drunk and took the pussy from me. Those cries in the shower be something else.

"Let you do you? Do you? Please." Dolph scoffed. "And where you gon' go? Come on now, you know a nigga loves you, Ty. I'mma try to control my anger, aight? I promise, baby. You gotta stop doing shit to get me mad and shit."

"Get you mad? Dolph, you wake up feeling a way all on your own! It could be two in the afternoon and you'll start some shit up." I swallowed hard as the tears started to roll down my cheeks. Looking at this man through my one good eye, I just shook my head and whispered, "I can't. I can't do this anymore. Please...I deserve so much better than this. You promised me you would never hurt me. I can't do this shit anymore, Dolph. Just let me leave, man."

He moved closer to me and my heart started pounding. I was scared as shit. He leaned over so he was right in my face and said, "Listen, fuck all that shit you kicking. On God, you got me fucked up right now. I was supposed to be taking care of shit for my party but nah, a nigga in this muthafucking funky ass hospital with your ass and gotta delay shit. You think my time and my money's a game?"

"That's all you fucking care about. Drugs and your money!"

"Bitch, I care about your dumb ass too!" Dolph hollered then checked himself and flexed his jawline. "Tell me something, beautiful, what nigga gon' love you besides me, huh? Haven't I been the only muthafucka that's been there for you and taking care of you and your fucking mother? This is the shit you gon' pull, call yourself wanting leave? Nah, I suggest you shake this shit off and act like you know better, you hear me? If you ever think about leaving a nigga again, bitch, I promise you I'mma kill your ass for real for real."

I felt disgusted by what this nigga was whispering to me. How could the one who was supposed to love and cherish me cause this much turmoil? How the fuck could this really be my life right now? I stared up at this sick and twisted muthafucka sad as fuck nobody else had come for me. Nobody probably even knew what had happened to me. I felt so alone. I just wanted anybody else to be in the room with me right now. Dolph kissed my forehead.

"You know I love you, right?" He glared at me until I swallowed hard and gave him the reply he was looking for.

"I love you too," I mumbled reluctantly.

He winked at me and started to walk towards the door. "I'll see you tomorrow." Without saying another word, he left the room, never bothering to ask where the flowers or teddy bear came from. Dolph didn't give a fuck about shit. All he cared about was making sure my ass didn't go anywhere.

***

After a lot of rest and observation of me and the twins, I was finally able to be released from the hospital later the next evening after three whole days. Given that it was the end of December, the cold air smacked me in the face as I walked out of Mass General Hospital. I was thankful my eye looked a little better and I had a slight limp to the right, but honestly, it was a miracle how good my body felt after the trauma of Dolph beating my ass and the car accident. I just assumed that was God's doing as well.

"You know, I just wanna say you're one tough chick." Nurse Laura chuckled as she walked by my side carrying the flowers, teddy bear and my duffle bag. She was the shit. She'd bought me some sunglasses from the gift shop to wear home. I definitely appreciated that. She said, "I've seen people come in here all messed up like you did and stay in this hospital for weeks. It's truly a blessing that you're able to go home so soon."

"Thanks." I smiled at her. "I just wanna get all the way better, you know."

"For the twins, right?"

I glanced up at her and softly said, "Yeah. Yeah, I guess." I didn't know what the fuck I was going to do about these babies, and I quickly pushed them to the back of my mind for the moment yet again.

"Oh, before I forget." Nurse Laura handed me a small envelope. "Here. The gentleman who came to visit left this for you."

I remembered what Gotti said about leaving his number and I just knew that's what it was. Looking around skeptically, I folded it and quickly tossed it in the duffle bag. "Thanks," I mumbled.

She patted my shoulder and lowered her eyes to look at me. "Listen, I don't know what you're going through, but if I can help in any way possible, please let me know. If you need somewhere to stay or...anything...tell me, Tahiry." The way she looked at me, it was like she knew exactly what I would be going back home to. The shit was scary. I didn't know if I should tell her I was being abused or just pretend like everything was all good. I started to say something when I heard a familiar voice that muted my words.

"What's up, beautiful? Thank you nurse. I can take her from here." I looked up to see Dolph hop out of his Benz to pick me up. Surprised was an understatement considering the fact that I just knew he would send Snookie's ass in the Bentley to pick me up.

Nurse Laura handed him my stuff and gave him the "once over". Without looking her way, I could feel her eyes shift towards me. She said, "I'll pray for you, Tahiry. Take care." Peering over my shoulder, I watched her walk away and back into the main entrance of the hospital before turning my attention back to Dolph.

"You're late. I was released an hour ago. I was about to take a cab."

Dolph glared at me and gripped me by the elbow. "I got tied up. I'm here now, right? Get in the car, please." He opened the door to help me climb inside then slammed the door behind me. He walked his slick ass around to hop in the driver's seat then sped off. "Nice flowers."

I dryly replied, "Thanks. A doctor's wife gave them to me with this teddy bear," I lied. I wasn't in the mood for the bullshit to start up so soon.

"Oh, okay then. That's what's up." Dolph cranked the music and sparked up a blunt. I cracked the window as he said, "I figured we need to talk and you could rest for the day. You know my birthday party is still this Saturday. You gon' be good, right?"

I ignored his comments about his party. I didn't give a fuck about his birthday. I turned twenty-one a few weeks back and to celebrate, Dolph took me out. First, he took me to pass my road test then we went shopping and he bought me a fat ass "promise" ring. Later, we went to a nice steak dinner restaurant on the waterfront by Seaport. Everything was going nice and smooth and I should have known some fuck shit was up. Sure enough, when we got home, he had our bedroom all set up with chocolate covered fruit, rose petals, champagne, lit vanilla scented candles and throwback R&B music was playing. The shit was nice and I was faded, letting Dolph pour my drinks all night. To this day, I don't recall letting this muthafucka tie me up, but I did.

That night, he let some random nigga pay him five racks to fuck me, talking about he needed a quick flip. I was kicking and screaming the whole seven minutes of hell that fat nigga pumped around. The second he was done and out the room,

Dolph unleashed the handcuffs and I was ready for war. I started smacking and punching him, cussing his ass out. No other words could describe how I felt besides cheap and dirty. He ended up getting the best of me and I was knocked out for a whole day. I woke up to a busted lip and a set of keys to the brand new Porsche that I fucked up the other day. Most bitches would have been ecstatic for a new whip. And while I loved the car, I wasn't too happy with getting the car as a makeup gift for the disrespect he put me through.

Glancing out the window, I asked, "Talk about what?" I shrugged my shoulders. "It's always the same ol' shit with you, Dolph. If you're not gonna treat me the way I deserve, just let me go and leave me the hell alone," I spoke dryly.

"What? Ayo, cut your shit. You know I love you, right?"

Laughing, I told him, "No, I don't know. I know you love the fact that I'm here with you, that's all. Love don't hurt, Dolph, and you always hurt me. Look at me." I sadly shook my head.

"Maaannn, please kill the theatrics." He brushed me off as usual. "All I want is my dick sucked whenever the fuck I say and for you to listen to whatever the fuck I tell you to do. I mean damn, is that so hard? A nigga done did mad shit for you and you can't even act right. Shit, that's the least you could fucking do."

"Act right?! Do you hear yourself, my nigga? Suck your dick, listen to you and act right like I'm some kinda fucking slave! I want out!"

Dolph looked at me then back at the road while he ashed his blunt. "Calm the fuck down..." I started going ape shit in the passenger seat, slapping and punching him while crying all at the same time. Something came over me and I don't know... I just fucking snapped.

"I'm sick of this shit!!! I wish I was fucking dead! You don't deserve me!!! I fucking hate you!" I rained blow after blow on him and cried as Dolph swerved in and out of lanes. I was fucking him up.

"Oh, you hate me?"

"Just let me go!!!"

Dolph slammed on the breaks and my body jerked forward, banging against the dashboard. He slapped the shit out of me so hard I could feel my lip split immediately then he pushed me against the passenger door. "I said calm the fuck down! Now you know if you wanna leave a nigga how it's gon' go! I'm 'bout tired of reminding your ass, Tahiry. On God!" He barked as he placed his gun on his lap and stared me down.

I was crying and breathing heavy as shit. "Just do it. Just fucking do it! I'm sure wherever the fuck I end up is better than being stuck here with you." I watched as Dolph squinted his eyes at me and lifted the gun. I held his twisted gaze and swallowed hard as he put it back under the seat. Other than my heavy ass breathing, it was so silent in the car you could hear a feather fall.

He nodded his head and started to drive again. After a moment or two, he looked over at me with a wicked smile and said, "I'm glad you know you stuck with a nigga. What you tryna eat before I drop you off, baby?"

Shaking my head, I had no words for this muthafucka. I sat back in the passenger seat and didn't say shit else. I wasn't hungry. I wasn't thirsty. I wasn't shit. I was just numb as hell.

Seven

My mind was in a million different places as we pulled up to the house. Flashbacks from the other morning came rushing back to me and I became weak in the stomach. Dolph hopped out of the car just as I opened the door and threw up something fierce.

"Damn, you good?"

I looked up at him then looked past him. There was my car shining and waiting for me, all fixed up. I so badly wanted to hop in it, drive off and never look back, but that was wishful thinking. Where was I going to go? Who was I going to run to? I felt like the only person I had these days was Big Mama. I didn't know anybody outside of Boston and Dolph knew mad people here. I was sure somebody would gladly turn my ass right back into him if I went missing. Mentally, emotionally and physically I was all fucked up and needed to figure some shit out.

I mumbled, "I'm fine." He lifted me out of the car and carried my shit for me as I limped up to the front door. He opened it and my mouth hit the floor. "Dolph! What the fuck?" The crib was a disaster! There was glass smashed everywhere, dried up blood splattered and it wreaked of trash. I couldn't believe this muthafucka couldn't even fix the shit up and really expected me to clean. He was talking about some rest when in reality, he wanted me to come home to clean the mess he fucking made. I should have known. "You couldn't have straightened up in three days? Really?"

He placed the flowers on the coffee table and just

shrugged his shoulders. "You know a nigga be busy," he stated nonchalantly. "I thought Snookie woulda did some shit."

I cut my eyes at him and turned to limp away. "I can't believe you..."

Dolph snatched me back and held me firmly by the waist. "I told you I could change your life, right? Don't you own designer bags? Haven't you been to another country more than once? Do you not live in a big ass house and push an expensive ass whip? I come home to you, right? Why is that not enough for you?"

Caressing his cheek, I smiled at him. "You come home when you feel like it and leave me in the crib alone." I cocked my head to the side as we stared each other down. "You'll never understand, Dolph. Ever. All of the perks of being with a trapping ass nigga is cool, but why the fuck would I want it if it comes attached with bruises, black eyes and broken promises? For two years almost, promises is all I've ever heard from you." My sarcastic smile quickly turned into a frown.

He flexed his jaw then sighed and kissed my hand. "I'mma do better, aight? I can definitely promise you that. I'm bouta go grab you a new phone today. See, a nigga trying."

"I hear you, Dolph. I just wanna take a shower."

"Aight. I'll be back later. I got some shit to do. And find that ring and put it the fuck back on your finger please." And again, he was getting ready to head out. Reaching into his pockets, he handed me a set of keys and kissed my cheek before dipping out the crib.

I put some music on and started cleaning the house, thinking about how to get away with murder. All I needed was something to knock his ass out with and put him to sleep. Or maybe I'd just suck his dick real good, slide the gun he hides from under the pillow and blow his brains out or maybe...

Two hours and a bomb ass shower later, I found myself in the kitchen hungry as fuck so I decided to cook me something to eat. I made a quick meal that consisted of spicy fried chicken, yellow rice and string beans. The crib was clean and peaceful for the moment. I curled up on the couch in the den and grubbed on my food before passing out. The sound of the front door slamming jarred me out of my sleep a while later. Looking around in the darkness, I was trying to catch my bearings, then I jumped up from the couch when I heard giggling. I knew it wasn't Dolph's ass sounding like that. The clock above the mantle told me it was 2:24am.

"Shit, Dolph. You heavy as hell."

"This dick is heavy too. Shut yo' ass up..."

The disrespect was real. I just knew this nigga didn't come home with another bitch, especially when I was fresh out of the hospital! Didn't he just say he was going to do better? I cut the lamp on in the living room and stood there mad as shit, grilling them both.

"Who are you?"

"Excuse me?" I questioned this bitch standing in my house at damn near three in the morning. She was pretty but I wasn't surprised; Dolph didn't like ugly bitches. I could tell they'd just left the bar or club by their clothes and the smell of alcohol coming from them both. I was black and blue and this bitch was holding onto Dolph looking like a doll and shit.

"Man, fuck all that. What's good with some head?" Dolph stumbled past me, holding the chick's hand. Immediately, she dropped to her knees and started undoing his belt.

"Dolph, what the fuck are you doing?" I lowered my eyes and glared at this nigga. "Are you serious right now? You 'bouta disrespect me like this?"

"I'm tryna have some fun right now and you standing

there bitching." He looked at me with disgust then lifted ol' girl's head. Dolph tongued her down then smirked up at me. "You gon' let this bitch have all the fun or you gon' come join?"

Here I was still healing from what the fuck he put me through and here he was, asking me some wild shit like this. I was fed the fuck up and charged at the both of them. I lost it. "GET THE FUCK OUT!!!" I grabbed homegirl by her hair.

"Get the fuck off of me!" She quickly uppercut me in the stomach and I let her hair go.

She didn't know I was pregnant but still, that shit pissed me all the way off. Mad as hell, I yelled, "You got me fucked up!"

"Ayo, cut the shit!" Dolph jumped in between us and pushed me backwards. I fell to the floor. "Sit down, Chasity." He spoke to her nicely then turned around mean mugging the shit out of me. I wanted to slap the smug look off his face. "Look, I'm tryna fuck, Tahiry. Is you with the shits or nah?"

I shook my head in disbelief and got back on my feet. "Nigga, are you serious? You just talked about you doing better but you ready to have a fucking threesome! When does the disrespect end with you, dawg? I really can't believe you right now, Dolph!"

Chasity snickered and Dolph let out a frustrated sigh as if he was tired of me. He shrugged his shoulders and plopped down on the couch next to her. "Welp...I suggest you carry your ass upstairs. I'll see you tomorrow." Dolph wrapped his arms around this bitch's waist and she winked at me.

"Fuck you, Dolph."

"Nah, she got that covered."

I stormed out of the living room and into the kitchen then snatched my keys off the counter and left the crib. There was no way I was sleeping in that house when he was fucking a bitch in my living room. I sat in my car, banged my head against the steering wheel and cried. I just cried.

***

The next morning rolled around and I woke up, still in my fucking car getting snowed in. The snowflakes were heavy, but I noticed Dolph's car wasn't parked in the driveway, which meant he wasn't home. I'd really slept in my car and he let me. He wasn't shit. I locked up my car and headed inside the crib. There was a brand new iPhone 11 on the kitchen counter and a stack of money. I wasted no time setting up my new phone and called up Big Mama to tell her I was coming over. I got dressed in some jeans, a long sleeved shirt and sneakers, then beat the fuck out of my face to hide this damn healing eye. I tossed on some shades, grabbed my puffy vest and my purse then left the house.

I remember the days I lived to get dressed up just to go to the corner store because I knew bitches hated me and wanted to be me all in the same. Nowadays, I barely wanted to get dressed. Today though, regardless of how my face felt or looked, I was out. I climbed in my car, took a deep breath and pulled off. I wanted to leave the house before I ran into Dolph. After everything, including last night, my chest was hurting so bad from the built up emotions.

I parked in front of Big Mama's house and hopped out just when I heard someone holla at me. "Tahiry!" I didn't fuck with anybody in Grove Hall so I was wondering who the hell was hollering out to me. It was freezing outside and I wasn't trying to make small talk, but I turned around and noticed it was Big Mama's next-door neighbor, Nevaeh. She was a young chick, a little older than me though, with a toddler girl always by her side. I never paid her much attention but when we saw each other, we spoke for a few minutes.

"Oh, hey. What's up? Hi, Niearra." I smiled at her daughter.

"You lost some weight, girl. You look good."

"Hi," the girl responded with a wave and bright smile. She was her mother's twin without a doubt; deep chocolate skin, big brown eyes and long dark curly hair.

"Yeah, well, you know..." I didn't say much and adjusted my purse over my shoulder.

"I won't keep you. I just wanted to talk to you about something right quick." Nevaeh put the little girl down. "Ni, go in the house with Meemu. I'll be right there." We both watched the little girl run off then she turned to me.

"So, what's up?"

"You fuck with Miss Sylvia's grandson, Dolph, right? He don't come by much but I've seen him with you a time or two."

Oh, boy. Was this one of these "woman-to-woman" moments and sis was about to tell me she was fucking with Dolph? The joke was on her; I didn't give a fuck. She could have a stab at the misery. I chuckled and adjusted the shades on my face. "Look, Nevaeh. You don't even need to tell me y'alls business. You can fuck with him all you want to." I started to walk away just shaking my head when she told me to wait.

"Girl, you got it all fucked up. I don't want him. He wanted me and when I turned him down, he threatened to have my baby's father shot at."

My mouth hit the ground as I stared at her. "I know you fucking lying..."

Nevaeh gave me a look and replied, "Shit, I wish I was. This was like three weeks ago when I was coming home from work one afternoon. I haven't seen or heard from him since. He's fucking crazy and I was just tryna hip you if you didn't know, Tahiry. That's all."

"Thanks, girl. He's a handful and I'm sorry you had to deal with that shit," I told her. "He ain't shit honestly and I'm just...

just…" I couldn't even get the words out. Why the fuck was I still with this nigga? Did he really have that much mind control over me? Did Dolph really have me that shook to walk the fuck away? I sighed and looked away.

"You don't have to explain. I think I get it but just be careful, you know. A nigga only gon' do what you allow and what you allow is what will continue, boo."

Damn, I felt that shit.

Pulling out her phone, Nevaeh said, "What's your number, girl? If you ever need to talk, I'll be around."

We exchanged numbers and even added each other on Instagram. I told her I would be in touch and we went our separate ways. I knew Dolph would be leaving Boston to head to Houston for his birthday one of these days coming up. I low-key needed to plan my escape from his ass. I needed to get the guts and just do it and say fuck the consequences and repercussions. I was kinda of smiling on the inside. Today felt like it was going to be a good day.

When Big Mama opened up her door for me, her face lit up and she didn't hesitate to pull me in for a big ass hug. The smell of whatever she was cooking up in the kitchen instantly hit my nose and my stomach growled. I couldn't wait to buss down some soul food!

"Oh, Tahiry! I'm so glad you're alright. Get on out the cold now. Why didn't you call me yesterday?"

"My fault, Big Mama. I was just tryna get my head together." I smiled. Her hugs were always warm and welcoming. "I got a little limp, but I'm fine. Thank you."

"Come on, baby." She motioned for me to take her hand. I followed her through the house to the kitchen.

Miss Sylvia Farrow, better known as Big Mama, could

cook her ass off and I loved eating her food. Unlike my mother, who knew how to cook about three meals only, Big Mama was a beast in the kitchen. I'd definitely picked up on a few cooking skills from her. She went over to the stove and stirred whatever was in the pot.

"Mmm, what you making on this Friday afternoon?"

"Oh, your favorite. I got the neckbones, cabbage, white rice, black eyed peas and some cornbread about to come out of the oven soon." Big Mama winked at me.

I smiled and licked my lips. "Damn! That's what I'm talking about now."

"Yes yes, put that smile on! You want a glass of wine? Some tequila?"

I chuckled. "What?"

"Come on now, baby. I know you need something, hmm?"

I sighed and shook my head. "Nah, I'm good. Thanks anyway."

"Well, shoot, I could use a little drink." I watched as she poured up a shot of Don Julio. Shaking off the strong taste, I noticed Big Mama get all serious on me. She looked at me like she wanted to say something, but the words were stuck or some shit.

"What's wrong, Big Mama?"

She sighed and looked away from me for a second. She swallowed hard then looked back at me. She said, "Tahiry, why do you keep letting my grandson hurt you?"

I felt like the wind had been knocked out of me. What the fuck did she just ask me? I'd always hid my bruises and the abuse from folks. How the hell did she know? I tried to play it off.

"W-What you mean?"

"Don't insult me, chile. I know Randolph is hurting you. I recognize the signs."

"Signs? What..."

"Yes, signs. What I don't know is how long it's been going on, but I know. Why do you women allow a man to hurt you the way he does?"

I took a deep breath and avoided her eyes before taking a deep ass breath. Looking up at her, I could see her genuine concern. I replied, "I don't know, Big Mama. I really don't know."

"Oh, but you do. Any woman in your situation knows exactly the reason she's staying in it. What's yours?"

"I don't know. I mean, I used to feel like I owed him," I finally said. "He-he-he came in my life and changed everything for the better. I mean, everything. Overnight I went from rags to riches in the blink of an eye and he made me feel good about myself. I felt like I owed him to remain loyal and solid and... but now...I don't know. I feel...stuck." I started to cry. I'd never told anyone that, but it felt good to finally release it to someone.

"Stuck? Tahiry, you're smart. You're beautiful. You have the singing voice of a goddess. You're only stuck because you're allowing yourself to be stuck." Big Mama sucked her teeth and shook her head. "How long has he been hitting you? Did he cause this accident? Dolph can be a mean bastard when he wants to be. He's been that way ever since his mama died when he was six. It's something about his anger that he just cannot control and it's scary."

I sniffled. "I just kinda started one day. I can't really remember what we were arguing over, but Dolph just started beating my ass. It's been off and on since then for almost two years. Big Mama, I feel like I can't leave him because then...if I do..." I shrugged my shoulders and lowered my head in shame. "I'll have nothing left." I broke down crying even harder as the reality of that hit me hard as fuck. Dolph literally supplied everything; a roof over my head, the money to buy the expensive ass clothes on my back and the keys to the fancy car I knew he would replace. I mean, anything and everything I wanted, I got. He was all I knew and all I had to lean on for...everything. Where the fuck was I really going to go? Who the fuck was really going to want me?

I touched my belly and whispered, "I'm pregnant...with twins."

Big Mama dropped her head into her hands. "Damn. All these years I've been wanting a grandbaby and here's two, but Lord knows not like this. You can't bring no babies into this situation, Tahiry. Father forgive me for even saying that considering the past."

"The past? Look, all I know is I can't stop thinking about it. These babies deserve a happy life and a happy mom, not a crazy ass father and a weak mother." I cried. "What am I gonna do? I know I have to leave him, but how? He'll find me. Boston is only but so big."

Big Mama lifted my head. She had tears of her own threatening to fall down. "If you leave, you'll have everything. You'll have your life and your dignity. But if you stay, Tahiry, that is when you'll have nothing left. Do you understand what I'm tryna say to you? You're such a good person with a good heart and my grandson does not deserve you." She stood up and hugged me so tight, I just melted in her arms, crying hysterically because I knew she was right. If I stayed with Dolph, I would for sure lose it all. My mind, my baby and my life. To hear his own grandmother telling me to leave him alone meant something big to me.

"I know Randolph is my flesh and blood. I took over raising him as best as I could until he decided he was a grown man at fifteen and left this house to sell dope." Big Mama sniffled and raised my chin so we were eye to eye. "Baby, you can do better. You hear me? Do better. If you wanna keep these babies, keep them for yourself and get strong. Boss up. If you don't keep them, do the exact same thing. Boss up and get strong. You understand?"

With hot tears running down my face, I nodded my head and whispered back, "Yes, ma'am."

She wiped my tears and smiled at me sincerely. "Okay... okay. Let's get you fattened up again." Just then, the doorbell rang and we both looked at each other. "I wonder who that is..."

"I'll get it, Big Mama. You can start eating."

I left the kitchen to answer the door and was surprised to see my mother standing there. She and Big Mama didn't really vibe well. Neither of them ever stated there was an issue but it was something. I think it was because over time, I leaned more on Big Mama than my own mother. I confided in her more than my own mother. My mother couldn't stand it but what could she say, shit had changed.

"Ma, what you doing here?" She was dressed like she was going to have brunch with the president or some shit, all elegant and shit. I'm telling you, money can really change a person.

"Excuse me?" She stepped inside and snatched off her big ass expensive sunglasses. "What are *you* doing here? I haven't talked to you in weeks since your birthday and I just had to find out about your car accident from Dolph. You couldn't even come see your *own* mother?"

"I woulda called you from the hospital, but I figured you were busy anyway." I folded my arms across my chest.

"Well, hello, Denise. How are you?" Big Mama greeted my mother politely but the tension could be felt all through the foyer.

My mother eyeballed her and dryly replied, "Sylvia." She turned to me. "Is there somewhere we can speak privately?"

"Listen, Denise, and I say this with all due respect to you as her mother, but this is my house. You can say what you gotta say right here and right now."

"Look-"

"Nah, hold up. Can y'all stop? Damn. Can we take this outside please?" I rolled my eyes. "Big Mama, just gimme a few minutes, alright?"

"You sure, baby?"

"Yes, she's sure!" My mother barked and stepped onto the porch.

"Tahiry, you know what..."

"I'm sorry, Big Mama. You know how she is these days. Lemme just see what's so important, alright?" I kissed her cheek and followed my mother outside. "Ma, you need to learn some respect when you come to someone's house. You taught me that, remember?" I leaned up against the railing and noticed she sported a worried look on her face. "What? What's going on?"

"Tahiry, I know you think you're so 'grown' and all being that you're twenty-one now, but you listen to me. You're gonna push that man away."

I twisted my face up at her, wondering where she was going with all of that. "Ma, what are you talking about?"

"Listen to me! All you gotta do is be patient with a man and do everything right. He'll love you forever."

"Oh, is that right? Well, what happened with you and my father? Because um... y'all ain't been together in twenty something years." I cut my eyes at her. She barely talked about my dad and although I'd been meaning to catch up with him, this shit with Dolph had me on some other shit. Besides, my father was too caught up loving on his new family in North Carolina. All I knew was he and my mother broke up around the time I was born.

"Dolph's worried about you and so am I! Were you that drunk you couldn't focus on the road? Really, Tahiry? You could have died in that car accident!"

"Hold up!" I put my hand up. "Are you seriously gon' believe everything that Dolph has told you, Ma? I don't even drink all like that anymore. I sip here and there!" I defended myself. "He's a fucking liar!"

"*You* don't have to lie, Tahiry. And watch your mouth. He says you've been drinking more and causing issues around the house. For what? Why would you be trying to push away a good man? He's done nothing but treat you like royalty since day one!" She told me.

I jumped in her face, not even giving a fuck that I was yelling. My mother was getting me heated right now. "You think Dolph is like fucking God's gift or some shit!" I exploded at her. "You don't even know the half!" I was so mad, the tears just started to roll down my cheeks.

My mother looked at up me with confusion on her face and pulled me back down. "Half of what? Girl, what the hell is wrong with you?"

I threw my head back and sighed. "Are you really that blind, Ma? Seriously?"

"What, Tahiry? What's wrong?"

I bit the inside of my cheek, closed my eyes and took a deep breath. After talking with Big Mama, I knew I had to tell my own mother what was going on. It was evident she didn't have a single clue what Dolph was really like and I just knew I was about to shock the shit out of her ass with this. I wiped my tears and said, "Look, this is kinda hard to say so I'mma just say it. Dolph's abusive...in every way. He hits me, he talks down on me, he keeps money from me and he takes the keys so I can't leave the house. Sometimes he...he...forces me to suck his dick when I'm on my period. He's...slowly...killing me, Ma." Here come the waterworks again. Fuck. I was so tired of crying, I couldn't believe I still had tears left to cry after all this time. The last year and a half have been the most draining of my entire life.

My mother's face dropped and she bit her bottom lip. She looked like she was trying to digest all of what I just said. I searched her eyes for some type of sympathy, but she quickly looked away and got up from the couch. Walking over to the window, she stared out for a minute and sighed heavily as all hell before turning back to face me. We stared at each other and I shifted uncomfortably.

Finally, she spoke. "Well...what exactly are you doing that makes him behave that way? Could it be your drinking? Your appearance?"

Hold up...what?! "I'm-I'm sorry...what?"

"I mean, you have lost a lot of weight over the last couple of months. Are you cooking for him? When's the last time you got your nails done? Why aren't you keeping yourself up?"

"Wait, what?"

"I'm saying-"

"I heard everything you just said, but are you really asking me this shit? Seriously? This is your response?"

"I mean, he's a good dude. He's taken care of you and even me from the very beginning without thinking twice about it. He obviously loves you very much, so whatever it is that you're doing to make him...lash out...you may want to stop."

I was floored! Was my own mother taking up for my abusive ass boyfriend? Just like bitch ass Snookie, was my own mother condoning his fuck shit? Was my own mother looking at me like I was the one in the wrong? Of course I was losing weight. The nigga was stressing me the fuck out that I barely had a fucking appetite. I went from a size fourteen to a size four in no time it seemed, but right now, my mother had me all the way fucked up.

"Oh, hell nah! Are you fucking kidding me right now?"

"Watch your mouth, Tahiry!"

"Fuck that!" I shouted. "Matter fact, you need to leave... NOW!"

"Excuse me? Who the hell-"

"I'm talking to you!" I slid over and got in my mother's face. "How dare you? I'm telling you that he's been hurting me and this is how you respond? Like...like it's my fault? I'm wrong? Hell nah! Get the hell out!"

"Calm down, Tahiry!" She said in a hushed voice. "All I'm saying is, don't fuck up a good thing because the two of you have disagreements here and there!"

"Disagreements that end with his fist going upside my fucking head! Leave me alone, Ma! I'm done with you!" I snapped. I couldn't even stand to look at my mother right now. "You're only concerned with keeping up with the Jones." I eyeballed her up and down with disgust. "As long as your rent gets paid, your new car has gas in it, and your closet has the best clothes and whatever else you've become accustomed to, you're perfectly fine with your daughter getting treated like shit. You're a trip."

"Hold the hell up. That's not what I'm saying at all! Do not put words in my mouth! I just think you have it better than I could have ever imagined for you." My mother held me by the shoulders. "You and Randolph need to work out whatever the issues are and please, for the sake of everybody, do your best to be patient with him." She kissed my cheek and said, "I love you." Then walked down the stairs.

I stormed back inside Big Mama's house and slammed the front door. I let out a scream so loud and tossed a family picture against the wall. The shit smashed to pieces and then I broke down crying. It wasn't even my place to be fucking up Big Mama's shit, but I was frustrated as fuck. I couldn't help it. She walked over to me and helped me get to the couch.

"This shit hurts so bad, Big Mama. It's hurts so bad. I feel so alone and like I'm crying out for help but nobody can hear me. Nobody cares!"

She held onto me and rocked back and forth. "I care! You hear me? I care! I can only imagine how you feel but you've gotta to keep it together. Believe in you. Tell yourself, this too shall pass. You hear? As far as your mother goes, hmph... I wouldn't spend too much time trying to beat a dead horse. Her mind is made up and it's unfortunate, it really is. It's alright though. Your next move has got to be your best one, understand me? It's gotta be. You hear me? And whatever you do, just keep me posted."

"Okay...yes ma'am." I cried into her arms and held onto her tightly. This shit had to stop. I was so tired of breaking down and just feeling broken period.

Eight

After that shit with my mom, I chopped it up with Big Mama a little longer while we ate. She asked me if I was going to Dolph's big ass birthday party tomorrow night and I honestly didn't want to. Like I said, I couldn't care less about that shit, but when I left Big Mama's house, I found myself thinking about his birthday party last year. It was the day my friendship ended with Jalika. Can you believe that shit? My best friend since high school was gone and after spending night after night crying about it, her choosing to not fuck with me anymore was all because of me. I was oblivious to a lot of shit and pushed her ass far away. I jumped in my car bumping Summer Walker's new joint and sped off. Tearing up a little, I thought back to that day.

"I thought you said you were coming out, J. You know Dolph's party is tonight," I whined into the phone. "I don't wanna be here alone," I whispered into the phone as I finished getting ready in the hotel bathroom.

He was born during Gemini season. Dolph and I had been fucking with each other heavy for over three months. I'm talking morning, noon and night type of shit. When you saw him, you saw me too. Naturally, I had doubts after I let him take my virginity that he'd diss me but nah, he did the complete opposite. He clung to me like white on rice and cuffed me harder than a crackhead cuffed a pipe. We fucked like wild rabbits whenever and wherever. He couldn't get enough of me. I was his and he was mine. Plain and simple.

"Alone? Girl, please, his boys will be there. Plus, I heard some celebrities are coming through there too. You'll be lit as fuck. You

don't need me." The attitude in Jalika's voice could be heard so clearly. Our friendship had changed drastically. I was always up under Dolph or taking a trip with him somewhere that I kind of forgot about my own best friend at times. I would go days and even weeks without returning her calls or texts. It wasn't intentional; I was just caught up in the life with my nigga. As the months went on, shit just happened. Jalika and I definitely weren't that close anymore.

I tried to put her on with Kase so that way we would be wrapped up with balling ass niggas together, but that shit didn't work out one bit. He claimed she didn't "fit the bill" to fuck with a nigga like him, whatever that meant. So they fucked one time and he curved her ass instantly, leaving Jalika feeling a way. It fucked her up because she was usually the type to forget about a nigga, not the other way around. I asked Dolph to check his friend on that shit, but he told me not to get involved in their business. They were grown. Anyway, Jalika grew jealous that I was always out with the fellas or hitting the club with them. I was even bagging up the work and dropping it off to his corner boys. I played my part and I played it well.

Jalika would often tell me Dolph wasn't shit and she couldn't wait for me to see it. I thought she was bugging and just talking out the side of her neck with envy. There was no way my baby was anything other than the perfect nigga. Shit, he kept his promises and kept me laced in the best clothes, shoes and jewelry and even continued to bless my mother with some money. She'd met him one day when he dropped me off at home and she was just getting off work. I was nervous as all hell, but he handed her some dough, kissed her cheek and told her that her daughter was always good and safe with him. My mother instantly called him her son-in-law. We were both blinded by what he did and the way he could make you feel. He was the master at making folks around him feel good as well as appreciated. My mother didn't even care that Dolph sold hard drugs for a living, as long as her rent got paid and the bills were never late. Her closet was filled with designer shit and he even upgraded her old Honda to a Mercedes. Denise "Pookie" Monroe was the flyest cougar in Dorchester.

It wasn't long before Dolph bought a townhouse in Milton and moved my ass right on in. He said he wanted to sleep with me every night and not just here and there. My life was literally like something from a hood fairytale. You couldn't tell me shit! I didn't care who hated it or who loved it because me? Tahiry? Oh, I was definitely loving every fucking minute of it. The only thing I wanted was to share some of the glory with my best friend but the reality was, we weren't the best of friends anymore.

As I applied the sheer gloss to my lips, I sighed. "Jalika..."

"Tahiry..." she mimicked me. "Come on, girl. You know damn well I don't wanna see Kase's no good ass. Ugh, I still can't get over how this white boy played me like I'm some dusty ass bitch. I shoulda fucked with Snookie. Tuh!"

"Well, if it means anything, Kase did tell Dolph he was sorry for how that shit went down."

"And you believe him? Bitch please. A nigga ain't gotta show me but once that he ain't for me. That nigga ain't shit and you know niggas of a feather flock together."

I frowned into the phone and rolled my eyes. "What the hell does that mean? I swear, if I didn't know any better, I'd say you don't like Dolph."

"Honestly, Ty. I don't. At least not for you anyway. He controlling and thinks the sun rises and sets on his ass just because he's hood famous and got money. The fuck? He's still human and bleeds like the rest of us!"

"He's not a bad person, J."

"Nah, but he is though, Ty. You'd see it for yourself if you weren't so stuck up his ass all the time. I mean, this is the longest we've talked on the phone in forever. You're barely in the hood anymore. You only care about Dolph, Dolph, Dolph...oh, and spending all that drug money. Where y'all flying to next?" Jalika lit into my ass! "You stay brushing me off. What the fuck is up with that?"

"I'm sorry, J. For real. You my bitch and after this weekend, I promise I'll be around more. I love you, girl."

Jalika sucked her teeth and replied, "Yeah, whatever. Go be with ya nigga, Ty. I ain't feeling being left out anymore and I damn sure ain't bouta beg a bitch for her friendship!"

"Jalika!"

"Nah, fuck you, Tahiry. I hope that nigga's everything you dreamed of. Don't call me when he breaks your heart either. I'm good."

Jalika hanging up on me brought me back to the traffic lane I was currently sitting in. Cars beeped and drove around me. Damn, I wondered how long I was zoned out for. A driver yelled out, "Non driving ass bitch! Move, man!"

I snapped out of it and drove a little further up the street before pulling my car over to have a moment. I could feel my emotions building up in my chest so badly I had to let it out. I missed my friend man. Word on the streets was Jalika was fucking with bitches now and had up and moved out of Boston with one. I prayed God would let her come back in my life. I knew I'd fucked up and if I had a second chance with my friend, I was never going to put another nigga between what I already knew was solid. My phone rang and I rolled my eyes then exhaled deeply when I noticed it was Dolph's ass.

Answering the call, I said, "Yeah."

"I miss you too, beautiful. You out being good or do I need to send Snookie to come look for you?" He laughed like the shit was funny when it really wasn't.

I scoffed and looked at the phone. "I'm fine, Dolph. Don't you worry. I'm not running away...yet."

"See, that's that shit I be fucking talking about, Tahiry. You always gotta get cute at the mouth, my nigga. Why?"

"Whatever. I'm really not in the mood for this right now. I'm starving. I'm just tryna get some food." I noticed I was parked in front of a diner and my stomach started growling again. I'd just grubbed on some bomb food but these babies were making me crave some banana pancakes.

Dolph yawned into the phone. "Where the hell you at? I'm hungry too."

"Dolph..."

"Oh, you on a date or some shit? Yo', on dawgs, Tahiry, I'll-"

"Stop with the fucking threats! Damn... I just left Big Mama's. I'm not doing shit." I heard him sigh into the phone like he was getting annoyed. "Seriously. I'm sick of living like this! I'm tired of everything. I'm-"

"Starting to get on my muthafucking nerves," he spoke coldly and I got chills on my arms. "Look, I got business to get back to. I don't want you out too much longer, plus it's cold as shit outside." Then I clearly heard a bitch in the background say, "Dolph, I'm ready to go. I'm starving."

I wasn't even mad. I already knew what was up. I just couldn't figure out why he couldn't keep one of those bitches and leave my ass alone. Set me free, nigga! All I could do was let out a sad ass chuckle.

"Yeah, business alright. Bye, Dolph." I hung up the phone and hopped out of my car to go inside the diner. I couldn't wait to eat. "Table for one, please." I smiled at the hostess.

"Sure. Let me-"

"Make that a table for two, miss." I heard a deep voice say behind me. I turned around with my eyebrows scrunched up, wondering who the hell was that bold. He smirked and licked his lips. "I knew that was you, Tahiry. How are you?" He hugged me close, smelling all good and shit.

I slipped out of his embrace and titled my shades down slightly. "Excuse me?" And then it hit me…it was Gotti! I forgot how fine he was and I could tell he was cocky as hell. I looked him up and down. "Oh, it's you. Sorry, I'm not interested." I started looking all around as if Dolph was going to pop up in any minute. I needed to put some distance between me and this fine ass nigga. I faced the hostess, who stood there holding both menus, looking confused. "Just one menu for one person please. Thank you."

Gotti stepped forward and handed shorty a crisp hundred dollar bill and gently took the menus from her. "I can find us a table, miss. Thanks." He winked at her and took my hand in his. "You stubborn as hell." I had to laugh at how arrogant this nigga was. We ended up at a secluded table in the back near the kitchen. "Have a seat," He demanded and pulled out a chair for me.

"What do you want from me? I was just tryna eat alone." I folded my arms across my chest, mean mugging him. He wore a pair of a crisp white tee, gray jeans with black and white Jordans on his feet. He was fresh from head to toe, again rocking another Philly hat.

"I guess that's one thing that's changed. Now have a seat please." He smiled and I rolled my eyes and sat down. He sat across from me and asked me, "Why haven't you used my number yet, love?"

"I don't know, but I hope you don't expect anything from…whatever this is. I'm hungry and you're hungry. We're just two hungry people having something to eat." I looked over the menu, trying to avoid his heavy gaze. "After you feed me, I'll go my way and you can go yours."

"Who said I was feeding you?" He picked up his phone as it started ringing. My mouth dropped and he laughed before answering it. "Yeah, sis…aight bet. I'mma get with you in a few. I'm with my future wife right now."

I kicked his leg under the table as I blushed. "You tried it."

He ended his call. "Damn, love. What, you got a lead foot?" He joked. I started laughing at that shit and I loosened up a little bit. "Nah, for real. I'm happy you outta that funky ass hospital and shit. You look good."

"Please do not gas me up."

"What?" Gotti looked at me like I was crazy. "Girl, you pretty as fuck, even underneath all that make up and them dark ass shades." He reached across the table to touch my hand. "How you feeling?"

Feeling the electricity spark just from that simple touch, I pulled my hand back and cleared my throat. "Umm, I'm alright. Taking it day by day."

He rubbed his chin and nodded his head. "I hear that. That's all we can do." The waitress came over to the table to take our order. He ordered my pancakes along with eggs and bacon then ordered himself steak, mash potatoes and broccoli. I got a Mimosa while he ordered a cranberry juice.

"Damn, starting early, huh?"

Cutting my eyes at him while I sipped on it, I asked, "Are you judging me?"

"Not at all, love," Gotti reached for my hand again and this time we just stared at each other. He said, "You ever hear that the eyes are the windows to the soul?" He licked his lips. "You been through a lot with this nigga, huh?" His glare softened.

I felt butterflies appear in my stomach and once again, I pulled my hand away. "I'm not talking about my relationship with you. What are you, the feds?"

"I told you who I was. Gotti, love." He extended his hand

and flashed his bright smile. "Can we be formally introduced?"

I sighed and shook his hand. Giving a light smile, I replied, "That was kinda corny."

I found myself enjoying his company and that shit scared me something fierce. We both ate in silence for the most part, stealing glances at each while we both occasionally checked our phones. Gotti let out a loud ass burp and I shot him a look. He laughed then got all serious, staring at me and shit.

Wiping my mouth and pushing my empty plate away, I asked, "What?"

"Nothing, I'm just wondering how long you plan on staying in an unhappy, abusive situation. Let me help you."

And just like that, he turned me off. Wiping my mouth, I gulped down the rest of my drink and grabbed my purse. "Thanks for the meal."

Gotti grabbed my elbow. "Hold up." I shot him a look and he let go of me instantly. "I'm sorry, love. I ain't mean to-"

"I gotta go."

Gotti stood up and replied, "I understand. But for real, just hit me up." He reached into his pockets before peeling off some twenties and tossing the money on the table. He looked at me and leaned into me. I braced myself because I just knew I was about to slap his ass for invading my space. But I didn't. I let him kiss my cheek then he winked at me and was out. I took a seat at the table before looking over my shoulder, wondering who the hell this Gotti character really was.

Nine

My heart so cold I think I'm done with ice (uh, brr)

Said if I leave her, she gon' die.

Well, bitch, you done with life (okay)

Better not pull up with no knife

'Cause I bring guns to fights...

The day had come, Dolph's birthday party. It was the day before New Years' Eve so you know the vibes around the house were turnt. Weed filled the air, liquor filled glasses and music filled the speakers throughout the house. It was about noon when the madness started and fuck if I was trying to sleep in; Dolph didn't care. Kase, Snookie and a few other homeboys who kicked it at the crib from time to time were chilling, turning up, starting the day early. Rolling out of bed, I shook my head and yawned.

Checking my phone, I saw I had a text from Nevaeh checking on me and also a text from Gotti doing the same. I smiled and held my phone up to my cheek, remembering that kiss. I jumped in the shower bumping *Umi* and sang along with him on my mind. His grip on my elbow wasn't one that scared me although he did grab the shit out of me. He just didn't want me to walk away from his ass, but if he knew like I knew, he would stay far away from me. I was hella damaged and not trying to bring baggage to anyone, although he could have been a nice guy. Plus, I still had whole human beings growing inside me that I didn't know would ever breathe a day on this earth. As fucked up as it sounded, the idea of being stuck with Dolph forever didn't sit well with me. Kids would mean I would be in this life for the sake of them and dealing with his antics forever until he killed me or I killed his ass. But fuck myself, I was thinking about the babies. They deserved way more than the bullshit to come.

I started crying my eyes out in the shower. I was feeling so fucked up, I became nauseous. I jumped out of the shower and lifted the toilet seat, throwing my entire life up not just once, but three times. I spent twenty minutes throwing up and sweating my ass off. Fuck my life. This was really the fourth time this week I'd thrown up. Damn, a bitch was really carrying this nigga's seeds. I clutched my belly and just cried. Dolph didn't believe in using condoms and honestly, in the beginning, the sex was juicy and good. I didn't really want to use them anyway. I knew better though and as the abuse continued and I noticed the other bitches, I should have made him start using them. Stupid me.

I struggled to stand up just as the bathroom door flew open and in stumbled Dolph with a blunt hanging from his mouth. He was fumbling with the zipper on his jeans, ready to take a piss.

"Damn, baby, you aight? Shit, it's colder than a bitter bitch's heart outside. The fuck...Watch out. Ahh, shit..." I barely had time to slide over before he started pissing in the toilet.

Wiping my mouth, I frowned. "I'm not really feeling good all of a sudden, Dolph. I just threw up. I think I'mma go lay down." I tried to get off the floor but was too weak. He finished taking a piss and helped me up off the floor. I leaned against the bathroom sink, wiped my mouth and sweat beads from my forehead. I was just feeling good and now here, I was feeling all broken down and probably looked like a hot mess.

"What?" He ashed the blunt in the toilet and flushed before placing it on the sink. "I got some people coming here to do your hair and makeup and shit. We 'posed to be taking pictures and shit, beautiful. Chop, chop." He started walking towards the door.

"No, now's not a good time. I just honestly wanna lay down and take a nap or something." I climbed back in the shower, hoping the music blasting would tune his ass out.

"And fuck up the vibe on my day?" Dolph scoffed and snatched the shower curtain back. "Nah, I can't have that so just finish up and get ready to meet the makeup bitch in the guest bedroom," he told me then squinted his eyes at me. He was so drunk he could barely stand up straight. Licking his lips, he said, "Damn, I might wanna stick this dick up in you right quick."

The thought almost made me throw up again, but I said, "Aren't we gon' be late? Just…"

"Yo' what's up with you?"

I sighed and turned the water off then stepped out of the shower. Wrapping my towel round me, I just shrugged my shoulders. I decided to come clean and deal with the consequences to come. Fuck it, it was now or later, and I was only getting more pregnant by the day. I looked up at him and said, "I'm pregnant, Dolph." I searched his eyes for the doubt and uneasiness I knew would be there. Surprisingly, I found joy instead.

He started cheesing hard as fuck. "You serious, Tahiry? Say on dawgs. You carrying my seed? Finally! A nigga been nutting in you like crazy. Ayeee, my baby's pregnant!" He kissed all over my face and hugged me tight.

"You… you're… wait a minute. You're… happy about this?" I thought I was bugging when I heard the excitement dripping from his voice. Yeah, like I said, we never used condoms, but Dolph never mentioned having kids and neither did I. I never even had a pregnancy scare in the last year and a half. This was the first and I was indeed scared as shit. This nigga picked me up and spun me around, kissing all on me.

He put me down and dropped to his knees, palming and kissing all on my belly. "Hell yeah, I'm happy as shit. I was starting to think ya pussy was broken or some shit." Dolph stood up and hugged me tightly. "You had had me thinking you done had an abortion before and was all fucked up down there. It took you long enough. I always knew when I got you that you wasn't going nowhere, beautiful. And now you really bouta have my baby. Oh yeah, it's official. You stuck with a nigga." He tongued me down aggressively and sucked on my bottom lip. This reaction would be normal if he was normal. Dolph was crazy as shit and to see him so happy to hear I was pregnant had me sick. My stomach was literally turning. I felt trapped. There was no way I was having this nigga's kids. Either he was going to have to stomp them the fuck out of me or they was being sucked out while I laid back on the table.

I pushed him away slightly. I couldn't wrap my head around this shit. "Dolph, we ain't even on the right track to be bringing kids in this shit. What are you thinking?"

He cocked his head back and looked at me like I was crazy. "What are *you* thinking?" He backed me up against the wall with this hot ass Remy breath in my face. "Please don't tell me what I think you're tryna tell me." He looked into my eyes.

"I'm just saying." I placed my hands on his chest, gently trying to calm the beast within and reason with him. "If we wanna be together forever then I think we need to work on us first before we bring kids into this. Look at what we just went through. That needs to be the last time, Dolph. I'm serious." I smiled at him. "If you love me, really wanna change and make this work, let's focus on us right now. There's plenty of time for babies, right?"

Dolph shook me off and slammed his hands against the wall. "So-so, you just wanna, uh... kill a niggas seed? Is that it?

You wanna do that to me, beautiful?" A lonely tear fell from Dolph's eye as he glared at me with a weird look on his face.

"Dolph, I just..."

"Sshhh..." He placed a finger up to my lips and shook his head. There was several moments of silence in the bathroom. He sniffled, wiped his face and reached for the blunt on the sink. Rubbing his hands over his face again, he turned to look at me and said, "Finish up. Lemme go make sure this makeup bitch is still on her way. We can talk about this later, aight?" He leaned over and placed a soft kiss on my lips and slapped my ass.

This nigga was crazy as shit. I threw my head back and slapped myself in the forehead. I could kick myself for this shit. I hated that I wanted to kill my babies, but I just knew God would understand. It wasn't supposed to happen like this. Shit wasn't supposed to be like this. I sunk to the floor, crying into my hands. Maybe Jalika was right to diss me when she said I was moving too fast with Dolph. He sucked me in from the beginning and I play right along, young, dumb and blinded. I knew I could do better than just being a drug dealer's main chick, but he promised me the world. It was like all my worries disappeared and a part of my dreams came true overnight. I had everything I'd ever wanted plus more and my knight in hood armor. I had no idea it was just smoke and mirrors.

Now I was knocked up and although it's not something I was necessarily happy about, I knew what had to be done. I needed to get an abortion and get the fuck away from Dolph. Period. That's what I needed and what I wanted. But when the bathroom door came flying open and Dolph grabbed me up off the floor by the neck, it became evident that what I wanted didn't matter anymore.

"ARE YOU FUCKING CRAZY?! HUH?!"

"Dolph!" My eyes became wide with fear. I clawed at his hand. I couldn't breathe for shit. I should have seen this bullshit coming. His ass walked out of the bathroom too fucking calm.

He continued to yell in my face. "After everything I've done for ya broke ass and ya bitching ass mama, you wanna repay me by killing my muthafucking baby? Huh? You wasn't shit when I found you and you ain't shit without me, but you wanna do me like this!! Ohhh, you must be fucking around on me and you don't know if the baby's mine, huh? That's what's this is all about, huh, Tahiry?" His ass was looking crazier and crazier by the second and talking crazy too. His eyes were dark and he was foaming at the mouth. He was really tripping the fuck out!

"Get... off..." I struggled to say. It was getting harder and harder and harder to breathe. I was seeing double. I couldn't believe what was happening. He could switch up at the blink of an eye. I was so tired of this shit.

I kicked him in the nuts and he let me go. I coughed my ass off and watched him kneel over in pain. I was tired of fighting with this piece of shit.

"Somebody help me!!!" I shouted, trying to get past him to unlock the bathroom door.

Dolph stumbled behind me and gripped the back of my hair, banging my head against the door. "Fucking answer me, Tahiry!" He growled and it was like he was connecting imaginary dots in his head or some shit. "Yeah, you must be fucking around on me, bitch! How dare you?" I had chills down my spine. I was scared as hell and once again, nobody came to my rescue. He slammed me up against the bathroom wall and the beautiful picture that hung came crashing down. "If you out here disrespecting me, I'll-"

"Yo', bro! You good in there?" I heard Kase holler as he knocked on the bathroom door a couple of times. Thank God.

"Leave me the fuck alone right now! Fuck!" Dolph barked.

I started to push him when he slapped me down to the cold bathroom floor then gripped my hair so I could look up at him. "If the thought of you getting an abortion even crosses your mind after tonight, I'mma fucking lose my mind, Tahiry," he said that shit as if he hadn't already lost that shit.

I was shivering and crying my ass off so badly, I could barely see through the tears. I was shaking like a stripper on her first night hitting the stage. My heart was about to thump out of my chest. What the fuck dawg? I crawled away from him and curled up against the tub, holding my head and rocking back and forth.

"I hate you. I swear, I do."

Dolph stood above me, looking at me like I disgusted him all of a sudden. "Clean yourself up and if I gotta tell you again to put that ring back on, there's gonna be a bigger problem. Now like I said, we'll revisit this topic in the morning, and hopefully you're thinking clearer. I love you too."

Out the corner of my eyes, I watched as he waltzed his ass out of the bathroom with his blunt and his drunken swagger. He didn't love me. Maybe in the beginning. And yeah, I might have loved him then too, but shortly after and now, I hated Randolph. My thoughts traveled way back to when he beat the shit out of that old man in Mission that day. That same person was who just beat me yet again. He wasn't shit. He said I was safe with him. He promised he would never hurt me. Time and time again, Dolph told me he would never throw what he does for me in my face. He promised me. I laid on the bathroom floor asking God why this kept happening to me.

**

Have you ever looked alive but on the inside, you were slowly dying? Shit, that was me as I sat by the bar in Venu tired and sore as hell but looking like a million dollars. Dolph rented out the whole club and even though I wasn't in the mood for the shit, it was a dope turn out. He legit brought the whole city of Boston out for his birthday. We matched each other's fly and the envious stares couldn't be missed. Dolph's black and customized gold kicks complimented the stilettoes on my feet and skintight gold dress that I wore.

The hair and makeup chicks that Dolph hired had me sitting too fucking pretty. I'm telling you, you'd never know I'd was recovering from a car accident and another beat down. Anyway, Dolph showed me off all night, and I even spotted a few of his other bitches up in the club. I threw on extras as we posed for the cameras, danced in the crowd and hugged up in VIP like we were really all in love. The shit was sickening how much it was killing me to keep up the charade. Dolph was a natural at making muthafuckas believe shit was all peaches and cream, but I was fed up with pretending. I was sure he was going to send me home and end his night with one of the bitches I peeped at the party. Right on time, a little after midnight, the DJ announced it was officially Dolph's birthday and the party went wild. Not even two seconds later, I got a text from him:

Dolph: Snookie's bringing the Bentley around to take you home. I know you probably tired and shit. I'mma come lay with you a lil later, aight, beautiful. Thank you for giving me my baby for my birthday. I love y'all.

I slid away from the bar and wiped a lonely tear that tried to slip down my cheeks. I wished shit was different. I wish I could go back to the beginning and either walk away or put my foot down. Nah, I should have just walked away. I simply texted back *happy birthday* then put my phone into my clutch and wiped my nose with the back of my hand. I made my way through the crowd and was almost to the door when somebody pushed me down to the floor and something dark was placed over my head. I felt somebody grab me up and carry me over their shoulder.

I started kicking and screaming. "Put me down! Somebody help me!!!"

"Ayo, stop all that fucking yelling! It's not that serious!" *THUD!* I was thrown against something cold and hard, and I must've blacked out for a little while.

When I awoke, my hands were zip tied behind my back and I could tell I was still in the back of the moving van. "Please, let me go. I gotta pee." My body was started aching from head to toe and my head was killing me. The van stopped rolling and I heard a door slam. A few seconds later, the back door opened up. I thought my eyes were playing tricks on me when whatever was on my head was snatched off and I saw who my kidnapper was. "Gotti?"

"Yeah, it's me."

I was speechless. We just stared at each other and neither of us said a word. Butterflies invaded my belly when his blank expression slowly turned into a smile. I looked away and grew shy for some reason I couldn't explain.

"So, what now?" The nigga who must've thrown me over his shoulder questioned, sparking up a nasty ass cigarette.

"You don't remember me?" The chick in the passenger seat asked with much attitude on her face. She looked kind of familiar, but I couldn't say from were. I just wasn't trying to have an issue with these people.

Gotti unzipped the ties and pulled me out the back of the van. Hugging me close, he asked, "You alright?"

"Honestly, no. What the fuck is going on?"

"I'mma explain everything, okay?"

"Can you start now?" I rolled my eyes and looked around at the others as Gotti held my hands. I was shivering, so he gave me his hoodie. "Gotti, what the fuck is going on?"

"Relax, Tahiry. Ain't shit gon' happen now. You're safe."

"Yeah, we did you a favor. Be grateful."

"Mac baby, shut up." Homegirl had hopped out of the van with the other dude. Now they were both hugged up in front of me. Everybody just stared at me.

"What?"

She stepped closer to stand in front of me, so I squared up, thinking me and this bitch was about to fight, but she knelt down and asked, "Dolph's putting you through it, huh?"

We locked eyes and it was then that I finally recognized her from a vague memory of something that happened way back. I should have listened when I heard her yell out, "Run!" It was Dolph's ex-girlfriend, Britney. Granted I only saw her from the view of the backseat of the Bentley, she looked nothing like the smoked out looking chick I saw that day in traffic. My mouth dropped when she said, "Yeah, it's me."

Ten

Gotti was living large in a loft somewhere close to Brockton. I felt like I was in a thriller movie because the décor was very dark and mysterious. There was wall to wall glass, brick walls, cozy carpet, dark furniture and there was a fireplace going ablaze, giving me a mysterious vibe. I was looking around waiting as if the killer would pop out at any minute. If I knew Dolph, he was spazzing the fuck out and him blowing my phone up with back to back calls only told me I was right.

I switched the shit to *Do Not Disturb* just as Gotti said, "I'mma go return a few phone calls. Tahiry, you can sleep in the guest bedroom or I can set you up in a telly for the night. Just lemme know." He left out the room looking frustrated.

I mean, this situation was kinda crazy. The only reason I wasn't flipping out was because Gotti was a familiar face. He saved me once and here he was again. There was something about his energy and his vibe that made me feel at ease. To Dolph, I was "missing". And for all he knew and could be salty about forever was, he'd finally lost me. The question was, how the fuck was all of this going to play out? I knew I was safe for now, but I didn't even know my next move. As I kicked off my shoes and cracked my neck, I sat on the bed thinking *damn, what now?*

Britney leaned up against the dresser with her arms folded across her chest. We stared at each other not saying a damn thing. I was crazy as hell how the tables changed in life. She stood before me looking better way than before. Her honey

BABY, YOU CAN DO BETTER

kissed complexion was now blemish free and glowing, the bundles in her hair flowed with the slightest movement compared to her ratty wig and the jewelry she rocked gleamed in her ears and around her neck and wrists. I was speechless for a moment taking it all in. I felt like the bum ass bitch Dolph always called me with her right in front of me. She was in nothing special but still popped in a tank top, high waist skinny jeans with a pair of red bottoms on her feet, and she gained weight. She looked nothing like the begging loud ratchet chick from that day. Hmmm, well maybe still ratchet. The diamond studded sunglasses she slid off her face had to cost at least a stack.

I shrugged my shoulders and spoke up first. "So..."

Britney sucked her teeth. "Lemme guess...Dolph fed you some fairytale bullshit and you believed him?"

"Excuse me?"

"You heard me." She shook her head and walked over to the bed to sit down. "You look just how I used to, stressed the fuck out and drained. You're either in denial or embarrassed about it." I jerked my head back, ready to swing on this bitch when she put her hands up and said, "Look, I'm not the enemy, Tahiry. Dolph is and my beef ain't even with you."

"How do you even...?"

"It's a small world. Gotti was telling me about this girl he called an ambulance for and went to see in the hospital. He told me how he thought she was being abused but just couldn't say anything. He wanted to help you but you seemed stubborn and wouldn't move on your own. So, we just waited for the opportunity to present itself."

"To save me?"

"To help you, Tahiry."

"For what? Y'all don't know me..."

"Nah, but I know Dolph and trust me, you ain't gotta put on no brave face for me, girl. I see through it all."

Interested to know what the fuck this nigga did to her to make her wanna help me, I sat back and entertained her. "Well, since you think you know it all, lemme hear your side and why the hell we wanna cut all ties with the same nigga."

Britney laughed and flipped her hair over her shoulders and said, "First off, Randolph Farrow is the muthafucking devil, girl. I'm not stupid either. I can see everything he's putting you through just by looking at you and this...this... this energy you're pushing off? It's dark and saddening. I've been there." I listened intently and watched as the tears started to roll down her face. It threw me off, but I continued to hear her out anyway. "I used to be you, only difference between you and me is Dolph got me addicted to coke and molly."

I looked at Britney, shocked as hell. "Yo', are you serious right now?"

"Yup, he does coke and sometimes lean, but hides the shit very well, and it interferes with him being bipolar. He refuses to take meds. Anyway, he started beating my ass randomly one night over something as simple as going to the club, girl! I mean, shit, it was a Friday night and I wanted to hang with my bitches, feel me? Nah, Dolph didn't want me going out and because of that ass whopping, I couldn't even go home to face my mother. He moved me right on in his crib, promising me shit was going to be sweet. And it was at first. The shopping sprees, new car, little getaways and shit then he trapped my ass with a baby. I wasn't ready, plus I was doing drugs heavy by then and trying not to piss this nigga off, so I ended up miscarrying. Shit went from bad to worse then. I was depressed as fuck with no friends around and my mother passed way in her sleep, probably from worrying about me. Big Mama never really liked me so I couldn't go to her for help and whenever I tried to, she closed the door on me. She either ignored the signs or didn't care." Britney laid everything on me and cried hysterically, telling me the details of her and Dolph's relationship. She was crying and shaking like the memories of everything triggered all the bullshit. I knew that feeling. I was triggered like a muthafucka.

I wiped my own tears and nodded my head. The conversation I had yesterday with Big Mama came flooding back to me. She mentioned she was able to recognize the signs and I now knew she was talking about Britney. Damn, this shit was crazy. Crazy because I finally had somebody who understood what I was going through because she went through the same shit. How the hell did Dolph get us? My mind was racing just thinking if there were other bitches put there damaged all from his so-called love.

"I swear to God, I feel the same way, Britney. Alone and just stuck with this nigga and nobody can see it. I'm fucking drowning!" I cried.

"Yup. It was just me and Dolph and his niggas of course. Kase and Snookie ain't 'bout shit though, just riding Dolph's wave because their asses probably scared of him too. He got the world shook because he can fight, shoot a gun and got money, but trust me, there's hella niggas out there bigger and tougher than his lame ass." She balled up fists while she stared off into space for a moment then came back to the conversation. "Anyway, I couldn't stop getting high for a while there, and he couldn't stop hitting me whenever shit wasn't going right in the streets for him. He would hit me and tell me he blamed me for losing the baby and that he'd never forgive me. He told me he couldn't be with no druggie bitch and one late night, I'm talking cold as hell outside, his evil ass kicked me out. Can you believe that shit? He got me started on the drugs. I ended up staying with this other fiend and got even more fucked up."

By now, we were both crying so badly, the shit was ridiculous. Britney continued, "Dolph would find me, sweet talk me into sucking his dick for some money, beat my ass and take the pussy from me. He'd only gimme like a couple dollars. He treated me like shit, like he never gave a fuck about me! It's always been about controlling me and making his fucking money!" Britney cried out and I hugged her tightly. "I'm pretty sure when you met him, he seemed like a dangerous yet nice little secure blanket, huh? Please! You were a fresh soul he could control. My soul and my mind were gone by the time I realized I needed to distance myself all the way from Dolph before I killed his ass. I just wanted to take a knife and stab him where his heart should be." I started crying with her because everything she was saying, aside from the drugs, sounded familiar, especially the thoughts on killing Dolph. I hated him for her. I hated him for me. I just fucking hated him.

"Oh, my God! Britney, I'm so sorry you had to go through this shit. Dolph ain't shit! I'm so fucking sorry, yo'." We both stared at each other crying our asses off.

She replied, "He was Superman in the beginning and made me feel like I was superwoman and the best bitch ever. Lies. All lies..."

Nodding my head 'yes', I told her, "He can't get away with hurting us like this."

She hugged me again and sniffled. "It's aight. It's okay. His days are numbered, but you have to leave Dolph the fuck alone or you're gonna end up in some serious trouble. No offense, but you already look like shit."

I wiped my tears and admitted, "I've tried to kill myself twice and I was just in a car accident tryna to escape his ass. I just want him to leave me the fuck alone!"

"He won't, Tahiry. Trust me on that. He likes what he can control and as long as you stick around, he'll slowly kill you. I thank God he woke me up one day and I said Lord, make me better. It's been about eight months since I ran into my brother and told him everything. He helped me get clean and got me a job.

Gotti wanted this nigga Dolph dead that same night we chopped it up, but I told him I'd let karma deal with it." Britney looked at me with all seriousness written on her face.

Glancing at my ringing phone, I saw it was Dolph blowing my shit up again. I turned it off and tossed it on the nightstand. "This is like the fifth time he's called. He's only gonna get angrier, but I just don't feel like picking up the phone."

"So the fuck what? Let his ass think you're really missing or dead. Shit, that could be your way out."

Laughing, we both fell out on the bed. I was thinking this bitch was crazy, but she might be on to something. Had it really come down to this shit? If only I could come up on some money, I'd disappear and move to a whole other state to start over. Boston was small and nobody knew me elsewhere, so the shit wouldn't be that hard. With Dolph gone, I could breathe again.

Britney climbed off the bed and we made eye contact. "Nah but for real though, we should let him suffer. We gotta hit him where it hurts and knowing Dolph, we gotta move fast. Get some rest. I'll be by tomorrow to check on you." We exchanged numbers and then she headed for the door where Gotti stood on the other side ready to knock. "Aight, bro. I'm out."

He kissed her cheek and replied, "Aight, don't get into nothing too crazy tonight, sis. I'm dead ass, I don't wanna get no phone calls."

"Okay, okay, damn. Later."

Gotti leaned against the doorframe and nodded his head at me. "You aight? Did you decide what you wanna do?"

Glancing down at my shoes, I knew I wasn't putting them shits back on. I said, "If it's alright, I'll stay here. Can you unhook my dress in the back please?" I asked him and stood up. I could feel his eyes running all over me and I got a little hot.

"I meant about that nigga. What's good?"

Holding my hair to one side to he could reach the latch on my dress, I replied, "I mean, knowing Dolph like I do, he's probably thinking I'll be home in the morning or some shit."

"Do you wanna go back?"

I turned around to face Gotti and he pushed my hair out of my face. I swallowed hard and shook my head 'no. "I just wanna be done. I want my life back, or better yet...a different one. I want...something better." It was hard to stop the tears that came, but he didn't budge. He held my hand. "I'm so tired, Gotti. I'm so tired..." He pulled me into him, rubbing my back as I collapsed against his chest crying.

"Let it out, love. It's aight. You gon' be straight."

I was sobbing like a baby with snot all in my nose and shit. I had the hiccups too. "How can you be so sure?"

He chuckled. "Eww, nasty, messing up my shirt. How about you let me worry about that? For now, just make yourself at home, aight?"

I sighed and wiped my face. "Thanks. I'd be lying if I said I wasn't scared or nervous or..."

Gotti placed a finger to my lips and shook his head. "I told you. I been here before. Britney was all fucked up and strung out too. That shit was crazy. I wanted that nigga Dolph's head from jump and even tried to one night, but shit got outta control and two innocent people died instead." You could tell the thought still fucked with his mental as he spoke about it.

"Damn, when was this?"

"Maybe like two years ago, a little less. Meek was in the Bean that night so I knew I would catch that nigga lacking." Gotti flexed his jaw.

"Oh, shit..." That crazy night I met Dolph came flooding back to me and my hand flew up to my mouth. "I was fucking there that night..."

"What?"

Shaking my head, I said, "Yup. That's the night I met his ass and been with him ever since. Niggas started shooting when he tried to holla at me and shit got crazy. He ended up driving me and my homegirl at the time home."

Gotti took a step back and gave me the once over. With his hand on his chin, he asked, "That was you? Nah, shorty he was with that night was a little on the hefty side."

I laughed and pushed him in the chest. "Fool, that was me!"

"Nah, say on dawgs..."

"Dead ass...I just lost some weight. You know, dealing with all the fuck shit."

"Damn, Tahiry. You was never supposed to be with that nigga, sweetheart." Gotti shook his head, giving me a look of empathy.

Still holding my dress up, I shrugged my shoulders. "I'll be okay in due time...right?" We made eye contact and he winked at me. Goosebumps appeared on my shoulders and I looked away.

"You special. God ain't saving you for no reason, love. You gon' do big things. Trust me. This is just a steppingstone."

"I appreciate that. Thanks."

"You got that. You hungry?" He started to walk towards the door. "I was about to order some food and just kick it."

Now that's what I was talking about. I wanted to pull this tight ass dress off and lay down, curling up next to some buffalo wings. I couldn't wait to eat and pass out. "Hell yeah. Can you order some buffalo wings with extra, extra mustard on the side, and a Cesar salad with some fries? Thank you." I twisted my face up when he started laughing. "What?"

"For a slim chick, you sure can eat. I like that shit. I got you." All I could do was blush and turn my face away.

He left out the room then came back with one of his T-shirts. He handed it to me with a towel, toothbrush and a shower cap. Damn, I wasn't expecting all that. I had a slick comment about his being prepared for bitches to sleep over, but I chose to bite my tongue.

I took a long ass hot shower, singing different harmonies and humming melodies that popped into my head. I made a mental note to write some lyrics soon. I was slipping. Once I finished cleansing, I moisturized with the cocoa butter in the bathroom and slipped into Gotti's big ass shirt. Creeping back down the hall, I climbed into the comfy looking bed and sunk into the sheets. Laying my head back on the pillow, I felt different. I wasn't on edge even though I probably should have been. I don't know what it was; Gotti made me feel at ease.

I hadn't even peeped he came back into the bedroom until I heard him ask, "So you sing?" He was bare chested, showing off a dope ass portrait tattoo on his chest with lounge pants and socks. The smell of his cologne hit me in the nose, and I forgot was he had asked me.

"Huh?"

Smiling at me, he asked, "You can sing? I heard you in there piping it."

Shyly, I replied, "I mean, I guess. I was just…"

"Nah, don't do that, love. You can *sang*. Your sound is different and just what I've been looking for." He motioned for me to follow him. "The food's in the kitchen."

Walking behind him, I noticed how strong and muscular Gotti's back was. He was bowlegged but not too much and his walk was confident and sexy. I found myself imagining my legs wrapped around his waist and got nervous as hell when we entered the kitchen. It was been so long since a bitch felt that spark I didn't know how to handle it. I took a seat on one of the bar stools and noticed the only way to calm my nerves.

"Is that wine just for show?" I hinted as I nodded towards the 19 Crimes Red Blend wine on the counter. I'd only had it one time and I remembered being fucked up off it. I needed a good night sleep tonight.

"Absolutely not. Crack it open." He winked at me.

I smiled and then caught myself. *Was I actually enjoying his company this much? Damn, I wish these butterflies would go the fuck away!* Shit, it was probably the babies. Come Monday morning, I was calling to schedule an appointment. As I poured us both a glass of wine and sipped mine, I pushed them to the back of my head for the moment.

"So," I said. "What did you mean when you said you've been looking for my sound?"

We started digging into the boxes of food, making plates and shit. The aroma alone made my stomach growl so loudly, I hoped Gotti didn't hear the shit. That was one thing about me; I wasn't scared to eat around a nigga. I wasn't all messy, but I damn sure could eat. Ever since I was released from the hospital, it seemed like my appetite kicked into overdrive. I wasted no time grubbing.

Gotti bit into a chicken wing and grubbed down too. "I can show you better than I can tell you. I'm into music and I'm looking for talent for this new label I just put together. You tryna be down? It can change your life." I was bussing down my food when Gotti said that shit. Dolph's voice popped into my head saying the same exact words to reel my ass in. I lost my whole appetite and pushed my food away. "What's wrong?"

I didn't say shit. I reached for the wine bottle for a refill and guzzled it down. "Nothing. I'm just not that hungry anymore."

Gotti got serious and moved closer to me. "I didn't mean to trigger you, if I did, Tahiry. You don't have to run from a nigga. Let's just say you're in the presence of a well-known, well-connected and respected man. You think that nigga run the Bean?" He laughed. "His time is over. Just gotta be smart, and I don't want Britney or you to get hurt in the process."

"I done had a nigga tell me he ain't tryna hurt me and he can change my life and..." I looked away to stop from revealing too many emotions. I was so tired of looking weak and broken for real. Plus, the wine was starting to make me feel sick. I knew what I was doing was wrong. Shit. Shaking my head, I said, "I'mma just call it a night."

Gotti stood up and held me by the waist. Lifting my chin so we were eye to eye, he said, "Didn't I tell you to stop running from me? I'm dead serious, I'm here for you. There's something about you that I'm really feeling regardless of what you going through. Everything happens for a reason. I can't help myself. I want you." He traced my lips with his fingers. Chills shot up my spine. *What is happening to me?* "Tell me something...are you happy?" He looked at me quizzically when he already knew the damn answer. "I know you're not."

I cleared my throat and swallowed hard as I felt us getting a little too close. It felt damn good but wrong at the same time. I was hiding from Dolph while pregnant at that. Shit was about to go from bad to worse and I just wasn't mentally prepared for it all. "I should go to bed." I needed to put some distance between Gotti and me ASAP! He spun me around and pinned me up against the fridge. I was breathing so heavy and my top lip started sweating. "Gotti..."

"Answer the question." He cupped the back of my head and started massaging my neck. "Are you happy? Tell me you're happy and I'll let you be happy," he whispered in my ear. "Tell me you're not happy and I can fix everything. I wanna do that for you." I closed my eyes and he held me close and nibbled on my earlobe. I started to get wrapped up in the moment, then quickly popped my eyes open and pushed Gotti in the chest as hard as I could. He looked stunned and I didn't care.

Holding my lips, I said, "I...goodnight." Not even giving him the opportunity to reply, I ran out of the kitchen and all the way back into the guest bedroom. Closing the door, I leaned up against it and slid down to the floor holding my belly. "Why me? Why?" Dolph always told me no other nigga would even look my way, let alone care about me. Here was Gotti, caring about my damaged ass from jump, not even knowing how deep the shit really was. I prayed to God I could get through this.

Eleven

"You bum ass bitch! You thought I wouldn't find you, huh? Didn't I tell you there was no escaping me? Didn't I tell you that you was stuck with a nigga? Bitch!" SLAP!

"Dolph, just leave me alone! Please..."

"Never. Ain't no nigga ever gon' love you the way I love you! This is my fucking family!! You hear me?!!"

"YOU DON'T FUCKING LOVE ME!!! JUST LEAVE US THE FUCK ALONE!!!!!"

"Tahiry!"

I jumped out of my sleep, pouring sweat with my heart pounding. I just knew that was real life. A dream ain't never felt that real before. Looking all around the room, I noticed Gotti standing there holding two iced coffees from PS Gourmet, looking at me like I'd lost my mind.

Wiping my forehead, I sat up in bed and mumbled, "Good morning."

"Damn, that nigga got you that shook? I ain't feeling that."

"Why do you even care?" I pulled the covers up as he walked over to sit on the edge of the bed. He handed me my coffee and sipped his, then just looked at me like he often did.

"Can I ask you something?"

"I guess."

"Why you so cold? Hmm? That nigga made you think you

was hard to love or something? You gotta ease up and recognize when a real nigga stepping in tryna make life a little better."

"I can appreciate that, but after having someone who I thought was prince charming sweep me off my feet then drag me through hell, it's hard to believe shit another nigga has to say," I told him, being truthful.

Gotti was cool as hell, fine as shit and genuinely seemed like one of those hood niggas who was loved on the right way growing up. He was respectful, kind and gentle from what I could tell so far, but I hadn't been a good judge of male characters so fuck yeah, my guard was up. After hearing Dolph drill it in my head that no nigga would ever love me besides him for so long, it became believable.

Sipping my coffee, I added, "I don't know. The shit I been through with this nigga makes me question everything. I'm sorry."

"Don't be sorry, love. I'm still here. I wanna help you and get you back to where you feel like yourself again. That's all. I don't want anything else from you," Gotti told me then with a smirk he said, "Unless you tryna get married, make this money and have some pretty babies with a nigga too. Shit, I'll take that." I started cracking the fuck up. He laughed at the shit too. I wasn't expecting him to say that and I definitely needed that laugh. "Nah, but we gon' figure this shit out, aight?"

"Why though?" I still pressed the issue. There was no way in hell this fine ass, grown ass man with his shit together was trying to deal with me and all that I came with. A blind person could see that I was damaged and going through a lot, yet and still, here was Gotti in my face, showing me he was here regardless. Given the situation, it was hard to accept. I just needed healing in every way possible thanks to Dolph.

Looking up at Gotti, I said, "You don't wanna get wrapped up in somebody like me. I'll only hold you up."

"If you don't stop that 'woe is me' bullshit, love. It's not attractive," he told me. "You gon' be aight, man. I got you. All I'm asking is that you allow me to help this healing process. The nigga gon' get what's coming to him."

"I ain't never wished death on nobody, but that nigga…" I closed my eyes and held the coffee cup tightly. "I hate him with everything in me…literally. I hate him and-"

Moving closer to me, Gotti pulled me in closer and said, "Don't worry about him no more. Shit's gon' get dealt with. You just worry about keeping a smile on that pretty face." He stood up, kissed my cheek and headed for the door. "I gotta run to the studio this morning but I'mma be back sometime early afternoon. You good here? I got food and cable and shit."

Chuckling, I replied, "Yeah thanks. I'll-"

The doorbell rang, interrupting me and he held up a finger to go see who it was. It was only nine in the morning and I was curious as hell to see who was popping up. Jealousy struck in my body as I crept out the bed to the door to listen, but I exhaled when I heard Britney's voice.

"Aight, later, bro. We'll be right here."

I jumped back into the bed and turned on the TV just as she walked into the room.

"Rise and shine, girl."

"Hey, good morning. You wake up early." I noticed she was dressed for the day with a head full of wand curls and heels. Yeah, I needed to get back on my shit.

"Girl, I'm always up early. Mac be snoring loud as hell for no goddamn reason." She laughed and leaned up against the dresser. "How you though?"

"I feel off honestly, and this dream about Dolph rocked me outta my sleep this morning."

"Whoo, I remember those days."

"How the hell did you deal with it? These dreams and flashbacks be killing me."

Britney sighed and plopped down on the foot of the bed. "Time. And Mac actually. I love the fuck outta his goofy ass. He came around when I was at my worse and loved me up until I loved myself again. That's my dawg." She smiled. "You just gotta give it time."

Reaching for my phone, I turned it back on and plugged it up. "Well, that's wassup. I don't know what the future holds for me. I just know I wanna be done with this nigga."

"My brother is feeling the hell outta you. I can tell. He's a good nigga but hella busy so bitches don't be sticking around, but he ain't got no kids and no crazy bitches after him," she told me, running me all the business. "Shit, he might be the one to show you what real love is."

I laughed. "Girl bye. I don't even know him like that and he ain't gon' want me. We just had that talk. I'm damaged goods..." My heart sank into my stomach when my phone finally turned on. I had texts and voicemails from everybody, including my mother, Dolph, Big Mama and an unknown number. It was ridiculous.

"Hold on," I told Britney as I listened to the messages.

"*Tahiry!*" It was my mother. "*What the hell is going on? Where are you? Dolph called me going crazy! He said something about you're playing hide and seek. Didn't we talk about this? Tahiry, I need-*" I deleted the message before I even listened to the rest. She was cooked. I already knew whose side she was on.

Next message was from Big Mama.

"*Tahiry, what happened? Snookie came banging on my goddamn door like a maniac! Dolph is on a rampage. That's all I know.*

Please call me. Please!" I saved her message and made a mental note to hit her back then listened to the other messages.

"Yo' where the fuck you at man? I just wanna talk to you. I'm not gon' hurt you anymore, beautiful. I fucking love you, Tahiry dawg!!! Answer the fucking phone, man!"

"Bitch, don't make me come find you. You know that shits possible. You must got some new dick already, huh? You gon' make me turn the Bean upside down for you? I don't think you want that."

I watched as Britney looked at me funny. "What?" She asked.

Putting the phone on speaker, I let her listen to the messages with me. Somebody else had to hear this sick shit. "Just listen..."

"What type of shit you on? You think you just gon' disappear on a nigga? You know a nigga love ya ass, bitch!!! What the fuck? Stop fucking playing with me and carry your ass the fuck home!!"

"You know what, I don't even give a fuck if you come back, bitch. You got me fucked up! You know how many bitches wanna fuck with a nigga? Wait 'til I get to Houston, them bitches are lit as fuck. You just a bum ass, pathetic excuse for a fucking female. BITCH!!! FUCK YOUUUU!!!!"

"TAHIRY!!! The fuck... my phone dying and some more shit. I know you see me blowing you up. I can't believe you on this shit. You really playing this fucking game? I love you too much for this. Fuck, dawg! I'm sorry for putting my hands on you, beautiful. Ain't nobody gon' love you how I fucking love you. You know that shit, right? You carrying my seed! We gon' be good, dawg!! Just come the fuck home. I'm losing it right now."

"Yo' is you fucking stupid or slow? Huh? Which fucking one, bitch? You sucking some dick right now or something?! That's why you can't pick up a fucking phone! On God, I'll kill you and that muthafucka!!! Keep fucking playing with me!!!!!

I couldn't even finish listening to the messages. Britney snatched my phone and tossed it on the bed. I was crying so badly, I felt like I was going to throw up. This nigga was fucking crazy and all I kept thinking about was my babies. If I went through with the whole pregnancy, how could I protect all of us from his ass? I didn't see this shit ending in a good note at all. I knew Dolph and what he was capable of. He wouldn't stop until I was right back under his thumb. I just wanted this feeling and the memory of being Dolph to disappear like yesterday!

"I hate him!"

"Fuck him! Tahiry, you're pregnant? Damn."

Sniffling, I just nodded my head. "With fucking twins! I don't wanna keep them and I feel so fucked up about it."

"Nah, you're smarter than that. It's fucked up, but you know what you gotta do, girl." She shook her head while rubbing my back.

"Ugh, this shit's just crazy, man. I never thought it would get like this. I shoulda been walked away. I shoulda been said fuck the consequences, dipped and never looked back." I cried. "Now, I'm gone, and I'm thinking I should go back to avoid the craziness I know is coming or say fuck it and push through the shit."

"Yup, that's exactly what you're gonna do. Suck them tears up and handle your business," Britney said to me, keeping it a buck. "I can't sugarcoat this shit when I say fuck him and his feelings. Don't be scared. You got me and my brother now. Whenever you go for that appointment, I'll be right there with you."

"Thanks, Britney. I don't know why you're being so nice, but I definitely could use a friend, so I appreciate it."

Laughing, she replied, "Girl, don't thank me. I been in your shoes and didn't have anybody until it was damn near too late.

I know what this shit feels like so yeah, I'm here." Turning on some music, she said, "But alright, enough of the mopey shit, I say we rob his ass. Fuck it. Let's call him up for ransom."

Sniffling, I looked at her like she was crazy. "What? Nah..."

"Well, let's go take your shit and his money too! Why not? He owes you and trust me, he ain't gon' miss the money. He doesn't know where you're at, right?" Britney looked at me with low eyes, and I could see the wheels spinning in her head. "Well shit, the way I see it, that's perfect timing." I contemplated on what she was saying and she continued, "Look, I say we go pack your shit up and take whatever money that nigga got in the crib."

"Now you know all of this is easier said than done, Britney. I'm sure Dolph will be coming home to check and see if I came back at some point." I rolled my eyes.

"I hear you, but it's worth a shot. I got your back."

"I don't know, girl. Your brother seems like he would know how to handle this shit. Plus, I'm supposed to be "missing". What if Dolph pops up and catches us? Then what, Ms. Know It All?" I gave her the side-eye.

Britney let out a frustrated sigh when she noticed my hesitation. "Tahiry, ain't nothing to it but to do it, feel me? Gotti's at the studio and told me to chill with you for a few." She gave me a smirk. I should have listened to my gut and kept my ass at Gotti's house until he got back but nope, here I was, sitting in front of my house, debating whether I was going inside or not.

I looked at the house and the glanced over at Britney standing beside me. "Nice house. Maybe he does love you," she snickered and gave me a nudge to the side.

"Shut up. I can't believe I'm even doing this."

"You're only taking back what you deserve."

She was right though. This was the opportunity of a lifetime to get over on Dolph. He wouldn't know what hit him.

***

"Ain't nothing to it but to do it, feel me?"

Britney's words replayed over and over in my head as we moved quickly through the home I shared with Dolph. We was grabbing clothes, shoes, jewelry, my notebooks, lotions, perfumes and whatever else caught my eye. My heart was racing as I filled the duffle bags with my shit. I couldn't stop the tears from falling. This was long overdue, but I was glad I finally had the courage and opportunity along with some help to set myself free of the bullshit. They say everything happens for a reason. Whatever the reason was and however the shit came to be, I was so grateful for Britney and Gotti. Closets were empty and the bags were packed. My phone started ringing and I almost jumped out of my skin. It was Dolph! I just let the shit ring.

"Fuck him. Let's hurry up."

"Wait, don't forget to grab you some dough, girl."

"Oh yeah..."

See, I wasn't too stupid over the years. I wasn't stashing money like I should have been, but I definitely kept a close eye on the safe whenever Dolph did put up some money. He kept one under the bed and with ease, I entered the code. My eyes popped out of my head when I opened the shit. Just like that song, there were racks on rack on racks of money inside with a gun on top.

"Well, damn!" Britney and I just looked at each other with our mouths wide open. The money made my mouth water, but knowing Dolph, that burner was connected to some bad shit so my ass wasn't touching it. "Watch out..." I pulled the safe from under the bed and tipped it over. The gun fell out and as I reached for the money, we heard the front door open and slam shut.

"Oh shit!" Britney damn near knocked me over. Our scared asses shot to our feet and went to look out the window. The red Bentley was parked right outside. Fuck! Maybe this wasn't going to be an easy getaway. "Who's that?"

"It's either Snookie and Dolph or just Snookie 'cause Dolph doesn't drive the Bentley." I started biting my nails.

"Fuck we gon' do?"

Thinking quick on my feet, I tiptoed to close and lock the bedroom door. The curtain flew around all crazy from the cold breeze outside and I swallowed hard. I knew what I had to do. I was going to have to leave the house from the fucking window. Wait, no. What the fuck was I thinking? I felt like I was trapped in a Lifetime movie with a killer in the house and I had to escape. Only it wasn't a killer after me, just a crazy ass nigga who would surely stop me from leaving. Nah, I couldn't afford that. I didn't want to get my ass beat again or worse. I couldn't do it anymore. I had to leave.

"I got an idea. Let's drop these bags out the window."

"And if need be, we gon' go out this bitch guns blazing," Britney said as she picked up the gun and took the safety off.

"Put that shit down!" I said in a loud whisper.

"Shut up..."

We started dropping the bags out of the window then slowly shut the window and crept out of the bedroom. It was quiet and I turned my face up wondering who was in my house and where the person was. Just then, as if somebody took the volume off mute, I heard skin slapping, loud grunting and moaning coming from downstairs.

"Ohhh yeah, fuck me!!!"

"You like that dick, huh? Bitch, play with my balls. Ooooh, yeah, just like that."

"Ohhh fuck!"

"Spit on 'em..."

"Tear it up, tear it up!!!"

As Britney and me tiptoed down the steps, this horrible ass smell hit my nose and must've hit hers too.

"Oh fucks no," She whispered to me with her face all screwed up. "Did this nigga bring a dirty ass bitch to your crib to fuck?" I shook my head and held my nose. I had bigger shit to worry about though. We needed to get the fuck out of the house!

"Girl, I don't care. Come on, let's go through the kitchen."

"Dolph, baby, breakfast is ready..." I bumped right into some white snow bunny wearing a robe, fishnets and kitten heels holding a tray of coke, pills and weed. Her eyes almost popped out of her head when she saw me. "Shit. Dolph!" I didn't hesitate to punch her in the face. Everything she was holding fell out of her hand as I pushed her to the floor.

"Ayo, what the fuck?"

Britney and I both froze in place at the bottom of the stairs. Dolph ran out of the living room with a hard dick and his boxers around his ankles to see the commotion and he damn near lost his shit when he saw me. I think he was more shocked to see me Britney. The nasty nigga didn't even have a condom on. He blinked and stumbled backwards. I could tell he was fucked up off some shit.

"What the...Ty...?"

"Dolph, baby, what's good? A nigga didn't even catch this nut yet."

"Oh, my God!"

This big, black nigga stood in the doorway of the living room jerking his dick off, completely naked. "Oh, we got more company, baby? What's good, ladies? Y'all joining in?"

"Hell nah! I knew you was crazy but fucking with niggas too?!" I shook my head, unable to believe the shit I was seeing and hearing.

"Bitch, get over here!" Dolph lunged for me, but I dodged him. Britney snatched my hand and we took off running towards the kitchen.

"Loose bootyhole wanna be gangsta ass niggas! Wait until everybody hear about this shit!" Britney cackled. "Ohh, it's definitely a fucking wrap for your ass, Dolph! Come on, Tahiry!"

"Dolph, what happened to Shelly?!" I heard a female shout.

"Not now, Nina! Tahiry!!!"

"Fuck you, fruity ass muthafucka!" I hollered back then started snatching the locks off the back door. POW! "Oh, my God!!!" His crazy ass started shooting at us but luckily, I heard the shit jam just as we burst through the back door. "Hurry up!!!" I yelled to Britney as we ran to my car. We both were breathing heavy as shit and sweating our asses off. Fuck the bags; my only concern was getting away from Dolph.

"DRIVE BITCH!!!" For some reason, of all times, the engine was sputtering and whatnot.

"Shit!"

"Girl, drive! Come on..."

"I'm trying to, Britney! This ain't never happened before." I pumped the pedal a couple of times then put the key in the ignition and tried to start the car again. No luck. I was thinking this was God's doing again, wanting to keep me stuck here by any means necessary. Or maybe it wasn't God. Nah, this was the devil working for sure.

"Ugh, come the fuck on!!" I shouted.

POW! POW! POW!

Dolph had made it out the house fully clothed was now shooting at the damn car. The back window came crashing in, getting glass all over the backseat.

"Oh, my God!!!"

POW! POW! POW! POW! POW!

"Oh hell nah! Fuck him." Britney rolled the window down and started shooting back at his ass. I kid you the fuck not, it felt like I was having an out of body experience. This shit was unreal.

"MUTHAFUCKAAAA!!!"

"I'mma get y'all bitches!!!" Dolph yelled.

This time, I noticed some neighbors had gathered outside but quickly went back inside when Dolph's big ass black boyfriend started shooting at my car too. The engine finally turned over and I stepped on the gas so hard. We jerked around as I sped off.

"What the fuck?! Shooting back at that nigga. Are you crazy?!" I checked to see if we were being followed and we weren't. Normally, I would have been mad that God saved me but this time, I was thankful he came through for me. *Thank you God for saving me again.*

"I can't help it I know how to shoot a gun, Tahiry. I told you what was gon' happen to get up outta there." She placed the gun under the seat, shaking her head. "Wait until Mac hears about this shit. And I broke a fucking nail...damn."

I sighed and just kept on driving. I knew I had to get off these main streets with my car all shot up. Granted that shit was just crazy, I was smiling on the inside. I didn't really care about shit else except the fact that I was free and there was no way I was going back to Dolph. He was literally going to have to find me and kill me, or I was going to die trying to stay alive and sane.

Twelve

"You did what? Didn't I tell you to sit your ass still, Britney? What the fuck, dawg?"

"Well, you know me. When I get an idea, I run with the shit. She got what she deserved and come to think of it, so did Dolph's bitch ass."

"Put Tahiry on the phone."

Britney handed me the phone with a look of annoyance on her face. Speaking into her phone, I dryly said, "Yeah, what's up?"

I was feeling nauseous as hell as I drove along. Gotti called, asking where we disappeared to and he started rashing when he heard about the bullshit that just went down. I just rolled my eyes. I wasn't in the mood for nobody's fucking attitude after what I'd just went through.

Gotti barked into the phone. "After last night, don't you think you should be laying low? I thought you were smarter than to do some dumb shit like that. You coulda been hurt and I already told you I'm not tryna have that shit happen! I need y'all to listen to me."

"Um, who the hell are you talking to?" I looked at the phone with my face all screwed up. Dolph was one to talk to me all crazy, and I wasn't about to have another nigga start off on the same note.

"I'm talking to you. You on the phone with me right, love?

I see you just as hardheaded as my sister." Just then, a sharp pain attacked my side and I doubled over the steering wheel.

"Ugh, oh shiiitttt!!!"

"Tahiry, you aight?"

I couldn't even speak, the pain was so unbearable. Glancing down, I touched my side and felt wetness. Everything around me was spinning and the pain was getting worse. I felt like I had to throw up and take a shit or piss myself. Either way, I had to pull the fuck over.

Gotti yelled again, "Tahiry, talk to me!"

Britney started freaking out. "Oh, my God, Tahiry! You're bleeding! What the hell?"

The phone fell from my hands and I threw my head back against the headrest. Closing my eyes to stop the hot tears from pouring out, I held my belly and whispered, "Fuck, fuck, fuck man...fuck." I repeated that shit over and over, then the tears just fell.

I wasn't stupid. I knew what this was considering all I'd just been through. Hopping in my car seemed like the only way to escape Dolph that morning of the car accident, and I'd just barely escaped him again. I did what I had to do and while I didn't take this as a sign of punishment or some shit, I felt conflicted because I knew this was happening for all the right and wrong reasons. With tears in my eyes and a heavy heart, I just looked up at Britney and said, "Help me, please."

"Gotti, we need you!"

She wasted no time helping me into the backseat then grabbed a blanket from the trunk and laid it over me. She jumped in the front seat and peeled away from the curb. I sobbed lightly through the pain in the backseat while she sped to the hospital while talking to Gotti.

"Fuck man! Bring her to Mr. Gee's spot. I'll meet y'all over there."

"Aight."

For a moment there, I caught Britney's eye in the rearview mirror. We didn't say shit to each other, but the look on her face told me she felt where I was at right now. Her eyes watered as she focused back on the road to get me to some help.

***

About two hours later, I woke up in a nice ass bedroom, wondering what else was coming my way that would knock the wind out of me. Not only did I miscarry, but I'd really just lost two babies because of the bullet that pierced through the driver's side of my car. I would have bled out if I was alone, but here were Britney and Gotti right by my side. Shit was crazy.

"Where am I? Where's Gotti?"

Britney sat by my bedside with a look of sadness on her face and said, "We're at Mr. Gee's, the hood doctor. Gotti went to get you some medicine. You need anything right now though?"

"Nah, I'm good. Thanks for...for everything though," I told her. "I really appreciate it."

"No doubt. I been there, remember? Only thing is you didn't have to go through this shit alone on the bathroom floor and have somebody scream in your face it's all your fault." We locked eyes and we both shook our heads.

"That muthafucka..."

Just then, Gotti bust through the bedroom door on the phone with a pissed off look on his face. "Aight, Ma, lemme hit you back." He ended the call on his cell and came over to us. He kissed Britney's cheek. "I see you woke up too, hardhead. Damn, Tahiry, you okay, love?" He dropped a CVS and Old Navy bag on the bed, and I noticed his face soften.

Britney patted his shoulder. "I'mma give y'all a minute."

"Aight, sis."

"Damn, just like superman, you're always right there, huh?" I scoffed. I didn't mean for it to sound so rude, but suddenly, I was feeling embarrassed and dirty about my situation. I curled up on the bed, turning my back to Gotti. I just wanted to run and hide.

"Why didn't you mention being pregnant? You just lost mad blood, Tahiry. Shit was serious. What the fuck were y'all thinking?"

"I don't know, alright! I don't know shit anymore."

He sighed and came around to climb on the twin size bed with me then pulled me close. "Look, I'm sorry if you feel like all niggas are bad niggas. You had one bad one, but I'm honestly just here to help."

"Help how?" I rolled my eyes. "We see where y'all tryna help got me. Fake kidnapped and on the run from a crazy ass nigga."

"You got a fly ass mouth."

"Yeah, so I've been told. What, you gon' hit me too?"

"What?" He shook his head. "Yo', you're a trip for real. I don't know what you think I'm on, but I ain't that nigga or them niggas, love. I'm Gotti," he told me, looking directly in my eyes. "And the sooner your ass realize who you fucking with the sooner shit gon' start to go a lot smoother. I'm not tryna hurt you, Tahiry. I was the nosey one asking all the questions and shit 'cause I give a fuck. That's all. There's some Ibuprofen, sweatpants and a shirt in the bags with some socks. I guessed your panty size. Small?"

I just looked at this nigga feeling some type of way. I wanted to be mad but deep down, I was impressed and a little turned on. I couldn't be mad when he was saying and doing all the right shit, but damn, a bitch wasn't used to this shit. Breaking his gaze, I looked away and cleared my throat.

"Thank you." I sighed. "Seriously, I know I can come off as a bitch but I'm really not. I'm just going through a lot right now and you're a lot..."

"I'm a lot?"

Sitting up, I continued. "Not like that. It's just that you seem so interested in me and you see what I'm dealing with. It's like... why? What's in it for you? Then you say good shit that any bitch would wanna hear, and I've been there and done that. Show me something different!"

"Different?" Gotti jumped up from the bed. "Didn't I call the ambulance for you the other day? Ain't you staying in my house? Am I not standing in front of you right now asking you to open up your fucking eyes?!"

"Don't yell at me! See, that's what I'm talking about." I started getting emotional and snatched the sheets back to climb out the bed. Fuck this, I was out. I grabbed the Old Navy Bag and Gotti took it from me.

"Where you going?"

"Gimme the bag, Gotti." I held the hospital gown together in the back and avoided his eyes while he stood blocking my way to the master bathroom.

"Nah, man, you always running away. Talk to a nigga! What the fuck I gotta do?" My phone ringing on the side table next to the bed interrupted our heated conversation. "Who's that?" Gotti asked angrily as he stomped over to get my phone before I could get to it.

I was nervous as shit until I seen it was just Big Mama calling. With all the shit that was happening, I'd completely forgotten to hit her up. I answered and said, "Hey, Big Mama. I meant to call you. I was just-"

"Ohhh now your ass wanna pick up the fucking phone 'cause you thought it was my grandmama? You really wanna play these games with me? Where's my fucking money? Bitch, I'll snap your muthafucking neck!"

I froze up and almost dropped my phone when I heard Dolph get to hollering all crazy. I couldn't help but wonder if Big Mama was alright. Was she listening to this shit? Could my heart stop pounding, so I could think for a second? Suddenly, Gotti snatched the phone from me.

"Yo' who the fuck is this? This that nigga Dolph?"

"Nigga, who the fuck are you to be answering my bitch phone? Where the fuck Tahiry at?"

"Aye, look here my nigga, your ass shouldn't even be breathing right now, so you might wanna count your fucking blessings. Next time, you done my nigga."

"Who the fuck is this? 'Cause on God, you ain't gotta talk about shit! Be about your word, my nigga. You think my bitch going somewhere then you got me fucked up! Both of y'all bitches got me fucked up!"

Gotti laughed into the phone and came over to tongue me down. A soft moan escaped my lips and I quickly covered them. "Uh huh, you hear that? Sounds to me she going somewhere aight...on this dick! Get the fuck on and watch your head, *Randolph*." My mouth dropped and I backed up from Gotti. He ended the call and pulled me close.

"Why'd you do that? This shit ain't no game, Gotti! He's a crazy muthafucka." I winced in pain and grabbed at my side.

"Stop forcing it and calm down. I got you. Fuck that nigga." Gotti lifted my chin and caressed my lips while staring into my eyes. I knew I looked a hot ass mess, yet and still this man was staring at me like I was precious jewel. He said, "I told you that you good with a nigga, man. Let me do my thing and you gon' be aight, just trust me." He palmed my ass and I let him kiss me deeply. "I told you it's something about you I'm really tryna fuck with. You gon' gimme the chance or what?"

I sighed and closed my eyes for a moment. His tone was even and his embrace was warm. I could feel the emotions dripping from every word he spoke. Everything in me was saying to let my guard down and be easy with Gotti, but everything I'd been through just wouldn't let me. I felt stuck, but I wanted to move. Looking at him, I replied, "The fact that you even wanna deal with me when my life is a mess right now says a lot about you. I like that but honestly, you just gotta give me some time. I mean, I just had a miscarriage for crying out loud."

"And I'm sorry you had to endure that. God never takes away what cannot be replaced with something better." Gotti flashed me a sexy ass smile and handed me the Old Navy bag. "Shit, take all the time you need. I'm not going anywhere, love. You can bet that." He winked at me and I smiled. Damn, he was dope. I stared at him smiling for a few moments, thinking to myself, *where has this man been all my life?* Then, my smile turned into a frown and I grilled the fuck out of his ass when he smashed my phone to pieces and tossed it into the trash.

"Gotti!"

"Man, fuck that nigga's service. You want him to still be in contact with you? Be my guest, but if I'mma be rocking with you, I'mma grab you a new joint and we gon' see what's good with getting you your own spot and shit, plus a new car." Gotti nodded his head at me. "By the way, you so cute when you get mad."

"Shut up." I flipped him the finger and turned to walk to the bathroom.

"Yeah, get your pretty ass dressed." He didn't say shit else to me. He just slapped my ass and headed for the door.

I giggled. I could get used to this smile on my face. I mentally kept my fingers crossed while I got dressed then met Gotti and Britney outside.

"Thank you, Gee. You stay coming through for a nigga." Gotti gave a brotherly hug to the old black man with the salt and pepper beard.

"No problem, Jonathan. You know you can call me anytime, my brother. Sister, take it easy, drink lots of fluids and get plenty of rest, okay?"

Nodding my head while Gotti held my hand, I told him, "I will, thanks."

Gotti told him to get rid of my car then he, Britney and I left Mr. Gee's spot in the hood to head back to the boonies. After all that shit, I was exhausted and just wanted to lay my ass down. On the way to his crib, Britney fell asleep and it gave us a chance to vibe.

Laying my head against the headrest, I asked, "So, why are you single?"

Gotti lowered the trap music. "Hmm, I'm surprised it took you this long to ask that." He looked over at me and I rolled my eyes. He laughed. "I'm single 'cause a lot of bitches don't like having a busy man."

"What? Now that's ridiculous. I mean, as long as you separate business from pleasure and make time for her, I don't really see the issue."

"And that's why I'm gon' wife you."

I chuckled. "Gotti, please..."

He gripped my thigh and I swear my pussy got moist.

"I'm serious, Tahiry. My ex couldn't stay down for the come up. She always wanted my time knowing damn well what I was in the streets doing. Then when I got my label started up, her ass wanna try to run back talking about history and shit." Gotti laughed and shook his head. "Yeah, her ass is history. I'm just tryna build up my company and rock with you to keep it a buck." He slid his hand into mine and smiled at me.

Smiling back, I said, "I hear you. Well, talk to me. What's your sign?"

"I'm twenty-six, a Pisces, and I'mma mama's boy. No kids, no drama. I done fucked plenty of bitches and did a bid or two. I'm wiser now. What's good with me and you?"

I started cracking up and shoved him. "Gotti, please. Just drive, ain't nobody thinking about you."

That was a lie though. He was still holding my hand and I prayed he never let go. He didn't say shit else though, just gave me a smirk and bumped the music. We dropped Britney off to Mac and headed back to Gotti's loft where he ordered up some lunch for the both of us. While he was in his office on a conference call, I ran a hot bubble bath. I tied my hair up and sunk into the deep tub. I needed this.

Thirteen

The Lord definitely worked in mysterious ways. Who knew me being "kidnapped" would turn out to actually be a blessing in disguise? Nah, I should say Gotti was really the blessing. The past three days were like pure heaven compared to the hell I'd been living in. Not to keep comparing these two niggas but damn, what a difference. In the short amount of time, I'd come to feel that Gotti was kind, patient, understanding and definitely about his business no matter what it was. Yeah, Dolph was about his money shit, but the nigga could have cared less about my mental or emotional state of mind at all. He was a tormentor and manipulator whereas Gotti was a protector and a lover. Let this situation had been different, shit, I knew Dolph's ass would have been trying to force something sexual whether I was cramping or not. Gotti was empathetic so he didn't force it, but the sexual tension between us was building day by day.

As I lathered up the cloth in the shower while Ella Mai's *Close* on repeat played from the Bluetooth speaker, I prayed to God, thanking him that I was slowly starting to feel somewhat normal again. Granted it was still being provided by a nigga, this shit was different. Gotti brought me a bunch of new clothes, shoes and jewelry. On top of my bruises healing, my hair and nails were laid and the rose colored Birkin bag in the closet had some dollars in it.

Gotti was right, fuck Dolph! The new phone and number from Sprint was holding me down. I'd hadn't heard from him and I was trying to be content with that. Maybe he got the hint or maybe he was sitting low plotting somewhere. Knowing him, it was the latter but after being around Gotti, I was confident Dolph really wouldn't be an issue anymore. He told me he would handle the shit and I was going to take his word for it. Finally, a bitch was feeling like she could let her shoulders down and breathe. Life was short and I was still young. I felt like Dolph stole some time from me, but thanks to God, Gotti, Big Mama and even Britney, I was going to bounce back. I owed myself a lot. This comeback was personal.

"Damn girl." Gotti knocked on the door and cracked it open. "You know a nigga pay for water, right?" He started laughing and turned the volume down on the side of my new phone.

It was crazy how comfortable I was around him just that quickly. His presence felt natural and the smell of his cologne hit my nose. I cut the water off then peeked my head out of the shower and frowned at his joke. He wasn't even ready himself, just standing there in some basketball shorts and Nike slides.

"Shut up, you ain't even dressed. Can you pass me my towel?"

I'd been staying in his guest bedroom and while we respected each other's privacy, we were both definitely comfortable together already. He told me he had a couple surprises set up for me today so I was a little excited. Our friendship was growing and the shit was cool. While he was at work, I was at his house chilling with Britney, writing or looking at apartments. I found out Gotti liked to cook, which was a surprise. I didn't feel pressured to cook if I didn't want to and he had a maid come in to clean every day. I felt like I was on a vacation and being treated like a queen.

He handed me my towel and said, "And you ain't gotta throw on all that makeup and whatnot for a nigga. You pretty just the way you are without Sephora."

I laughed and wrapped the towel around me before stepping out. He kept on saying that shit. On some Drake shit, he said

I was the prettiest with just some sweats and no makeup on. I liked to be dolled up. I'd become accustomed to it being with Dolph. So naturally, when Gotti told me he was taking me shopping, it was only right that I went back to my labels and shit. I balled out on some designer shit with mad heels and of course, I copped some kicks. But he was right. today I was feeling on a high and needed to be in comfy mode. I mushed him in the head.

"You act like I be cake face or some shit. Leave me alone, dawg."

"Aww the baby's mad. Look at the pout." Gotti smiled at me and hugged me from behind. We made eye contact in the bathroom mirror and he let me go. Coughing into his fist, he backed up and said, "You be looking aight but come on, love. You know Ideals be having that long ass line."

"I'm coming..." I smirked as I got ready to brush my teeth. It was almost noon and my stomach was growling. That tuna sub with some chips would be everything right now!

Gotti slapped my ass and left the bathroom so I could finish getting myself together. I went back to bumping my song while I got dressed in some white jeans, a white flowy top and some all-white Air Maxes. My hair was styled in long curly bundles that I decided to wear half up and half down with some big diamond studs. I grabbed my shades, tossed my phone and wallet in my bag, then glided some lip gloss on my lips. Leaving out the guest room, I met Gotti in the living room. Tell my why this fine ass nigga was standing there somewhat matching my fly in some grey jeans, a white tee and some white Air Maxes. He rocked a white and grey fitted and looked up at me with a smile, holding out his hand.

"Great minds think alike, huh, love?"

"Yeah, whatever. You was peeking at me while I was getting dressed. I ain't stupid." I tried to hide the smirk on my face, but it was hard. He smelled and looked so damn good. He pulled me in for a hug.

"Stop playing. You look good as hell. See what I mean? I like that natural shit. Embrace your beauty, Tahiry." He linked his hand with mine and we left the crib.

Gotti pulled up on a side street near Dudley Street to run inside Ideals to get us some food. It was almost eleven in the morning and my stomach was going crazy. I was hoping the line wasn't too long. I was still on alert for Dolph seeing as though he knew this was my one of my spots, but I told myself to chill and just leaned back in the seat. Pulling out my phone, I was about to scroll on Instagram when it rang. *Shit!* It was Britney calling, and I'd completely forgotten I'd woken up to her missed call and "CALL ME BACK" text. I was just amped to go see this apartment that it slipped my mind. Over the last few days, we got cool and it was almost like we didn't even connect over Dolph's ass. We just clicked in general and it felt good to have a home girl again.

"What's up, Brit?"

"Daaaamn, you too busy getting your back cracked by my brother you can't even return a phone call?" Britney sighed sarcastically into the phone. "Y'all nasty!"

I started cracking up. She stayed making jokes about me and Gotti fucking around so much to the point where I think she was manifesting the shit. "Here you go...cut the shit. We ain't even on that, girl. My fault for not calling you back. You alright though?"

"Nine thousand hours later and you ask that shit. Anyway, girl, tell me why I was in line at Popeye's on American Legion last night, grabbing Mac some of that nasty shit, and I overheard this pregnant bitch on the phone talking about a baby shower."

"Okay...and?

"Lemme finish...so, the bitch had the call on speakerphone and get this shit. She was on the phone with Snookie!"

"What?"

"Yes, bitch! You know I know. He's having a fucking baby and judging from the looks of this bitch, she's due any day now. I wanted to slap some common sense into her black ass! We all know Snookie's ass is a little slow anyway."

Laughing, I said, "Shut up! What did the girl look like?"

I listened as Britney described my former best friend to a fucking T. Only thing is, she said her hair was cut short. Jalika joked about hooking up with Snookie after Kase dissed her, but damn, the shit hit me differently. How long had they been fucking around? Wasn't she into bitches? When did she move back? Did the bitch ever really move? So many questions circled my brain. I was shocked to see hear this shit but happy I wasn't the one to see her that night. There was no telling how all of that would have went down. I was angry and curious. I needed to see what the fuck was up and I needed Gotti to bring his ass out of the damn sub shop.

"I know that bitch," I told Britney. "She used to be my best friend."

"What? What happened with y'all?"

"Long story short, we fell apart."

Britney huffed. "Hmph. Well, if she's fucking with anybody associated with Dolph's ass, she's shady, and the bitch was never really your friend."

"You think so?"

"Yes. So you wanna slap the hoe or what?"

"What?!"

"Hell yeah! Listen, if we gon' be friends, you gotta know I don't tolerate disrespect and now that you just told me the bitch was your friend, it's shady as fuck! I say we beat the bitch's ass!"

I couldn't front, I was pissed and I felt betrayed. Kase dissed Jalika, I had Dolph, so I guess she just picked third best... or whatever. Pregnant though? "Aight lemme finish up with your brother and hit you back."

"Ooooh, what y'all doing?"

"Bye, nosey!"

Gotti jerked the car door open just as I ended the call. He placed the food on my lap.

"Long ass line," he grumbled and pulled off down the street. "You okay? Sorry that shit took so long."

"Yeah, I'm alright. It's cool." I smiled at him. He always asked me if I was alright and I genuinely liked that. It wasn't annoying at all; it showed me he actually cared.

"Aight, greedy. I gotta stop and pick up some groceries for my mom's a lil' later. You cool with that?" This nigga took a big ass bite of his sub before cranking the music and swerving off.

I almost choked on my Lemonade. "Your mom?"

Gotti laughed. "Yeah, girl. Relax, she's cool peoples. My mom's my best friend, if I had to name one."

"Oh yeah? That's good." I started grubbing on my sub. "Me and my mother used to be cool until Dolph came long. I haven't talked to her since right after I got out the hospital actually."

"What?" He looked back and forth between me and the road. "That's your moms, Tahiry. Regardless of whatever bullshit y'all may go through, you only get one mother."

"You don't even understand. She's changed."

"And you haven't?"

I looked over at him then glanced out the window thinking about what he said. "I don't know. She's on his side. If I call her and she's on some shit…"

"Man, just call her. I'm sure she's worried about your ass," Gotti told me. Huffing and puffing, I rolled my eyes and pulled out my phone to call up my mother. Surprisingly, she answered on the first ring.

"Glory be to God…"

"Umm…hi, Ma."

"Tahiry? Where the hell have you been?!" Was the first thing she said to me and I just closed my eyes.

"I was just calling to let you know I was alright."

"And that's all? That's all you have to say?" My mother asked me angrily. "Where are you?"

"Why is that important, Ma?! Just know I'm alright. I'm sure if I tell you anything, you'll just run back and tell Dolph anyway." *Shit!* It dawned on me that I didn't even block my number before calling her. "Ma, please don't give him my new number. Please."

"Tahiry Monroe, I am your mother first. Yes, I can't believe he would hurt you the way he has, and I'm so sorry I didn't believe you." She started sobbing into the phone and it threw me completely off guard. "I'm disgusted and scared because he's been threatening to hurt me if you don't come back!"

"What?!"

"Yo', what's good?" Gotti whispered to me, tapping my leg.

Putting the call on speakerphone, I ignored him. "Dolph's been threatening you? Ma, where are you?"

"I'm staying at the Holiday Inn in Somerville off the highway. I didn't wanna risk him just stopping by the house again,"

She cried.

"Damn, Ma, I'm so sorry. Text me the address, okay?"

"Okay, baby. Be careful."

Hanging up the phone, I shook my head. "Now this nigga's threatening my fucking mother, got her all scared and shit. I ain't never heard her sound like that before. Something just don't feel right." I was so mad and shaken up that I was literally shaking.

Gotti took my hand into his and told me, "Everything's gon' be aight. You think she's being truthful though?"

Just then, my phone dinged, letting me know I had a text. It was my mom hitting me up with the address to the hotel and I told her I was on the way. "Why would she lie? She's in room 214."

"I'm just saying, you said she was Team Dolph, now she's singing a different tune and telling you to come to her. That's not odd?"

"No, Gotti. She obviously sees what I was tryna tell her. Dolph is the devil and content with hurting everybody as long as he's alright with his ol' faggot ass. Ugh..."

Gotti started laughing his ass off. "Fuck did you just say, love?"

Laughing back, I told him, "You heard me. The shit I seen at the house when I tried to get my stuff was disturbing. He was definitely having a threesome with a nigga and a bitch but somehow just fucking the nigga."

"That's fucking nasty as shit, Tahiry."

I laughed. "You're telling me. I was with the nigga..."

Not long after, we pulled up to the Holiday Inn and went inside to see what was up with my mother. The front desk staff were caught up on their phones, so we kept it pushing to the elevators. Gotti tucked his gun in his jeans and I rolled my eyes at his dramatics then texted my mother to let her know I was making my way to the room. With him by my side, I knocked on the door and waited. Nothing. Silence. I knocked again.

"Hello? Ma, you in there? It's me."

I jerked the handle and oddly enough, the door was unlocked. This weird feeling hit my stomach as I looked up at Gotti. He pulled out his gun and moved me to the side as he pushed the door open.

"Oh, my God! Ma!"

"Shit…"

My mother was laid out in the middle of the floor with her throat and wrist slit. I just knew this was a fucking bad dream and I was about to wake up any second now. This wasn't real. I ran over to her as Gotti closed the door and looked around the room.

"Ma…" I cried as I pushed her hair out of her face.

"All you had to do was stay down and fucking love me!" My eyes grew wide as I stood up and stared Dolph in his face. He appeared from the closet dressed in a black Nike sweat suit, looking crazier than ever. Before Gotti could raise his gun, Dolph let off a shot.

"Argh!"

"Gotti!!!" I yelled out as I watched him drop to the floor holding his stomach.

"Bitch, how dare you feel for that nigga?!" Dolph snatched me up by the neck and slammed me onto the bed. He looked like he was really losing his fucking mind. His dreads were wild and he hadn't shaved or gotten a line up. His eyes were dark and glossed over and his breath smelled like shit.

"Get the fuck off me!!! You killed my fucking mother!!!"

"That's your fault! Why couldn't you just act right, huh? You had me use her to get to you." Dolph started to cry and held the gun to my head. "I fucking love you, Tahiry. We're gon' be together and you're not gon' fuck with nobody else!!! You already fucking know!"

Somebody started knocking and beating the door down. "Keep it down in there with the kinky shit!!!"

I hollered back, "HELP ME!!!"

Dolph started choking me. "Shut the fuck up."

"I swear, you're fucking crazy...please stop," I managed to say as he strangled me. He tried to smack me with the gun and that's when I knew this muthafucka was definitely on something because he fell over onto the floor as soon as he swung his arm.

"Stupid, bitch..."

"Fuck you!!!" I stomped on his chest and kicked the gun out of his hands.

"Tahiry..." I heard Gotti whisper out to me and my eyes shot over to him. He was trying to stand up, but he was bleeding so badly, I just knew he wasn't going to make it. This shit was crazy.

A gun went off and I felt a burn in my shoulder, I realized Dolph's crazy ass had shot me. Holding my arm, I started to run out the room, but he gripped me by the head and slammed my shit against it.

"Stop it!!!"

"You tryna save that nigga over there?" Dolph raised his gun to let off more shots at Gotti. "Bitch, fuck him!"

"Nigga, fuck you!"

POW!

"The police are coming!!!" The person on the other side of the door hollered.

I don't know how Gotti managed to get up off the floor, but he attacked Dolph, the gun fell out of his hand and they both fell over onto the rug trying to get the best of each other. Dolph was winning. With my head pounding and my eyes full of tears, I reached for the gun and started shooting.

"Just leave me the fuck alone!!!"

POW! POW! POW! POW!

I dropped to my knees crying and shaking as I heard a body hit the ground.

The door came crashing down as police and hotel security burst into the room with their guns, flashlights and badges shown.

"PUT THE FUCKING GUN DOWN!!!"

"Don't shoot me please!"

"DROP THE WEAPON!!!

Standing up, I dropped the gun and pointed at Dolph and Gotti both laid out on the floor. "He killed my mother!!! He's trying to kill me!!!"

"Arrest her!"

I was tackled and thrown in handcuffs, crying my ass off the whole time. As I was escorted out of the room, I sadly shook my head at my mom and prayed to God that Gotti would survive. I don't know what came over me. I was just shooting and hoping the bullets only hit him. All eyes were on me as I was led out of the hotel. I was sure shit looked crazy and I couldn't wait to explain why I was the only person holding a gun in a room full of bleeding muthafuckas. They threw me in the back of the police cruiser and a female office rushed over to me.

"Miss, are you okay? You wanna tell me what's going on here?" She raised her eyebrows in concern and pulled out a pen and small notepad.

I looked down at the blood all over my clothes then glanced at the hotel before staring deep into her eyes. I let out a deep breath and just cried. Finally, my voice was going to be heard.

Fourteen

"Umm, good afternoon everyone. My name is Tahiry Monroe and I'd like to share a few words with you all." I spoke into the microphone and gazed out into the faces of the folks that sat in the crowd at Dolph's funeral.

You would have thought a celebrity had passed the way Morning Star Baptist Church was packed. The whole fucking city came out to see a "legend" go and even some news reporters were in attendance. The pastor, family and friends gathered and shared words and their love for Dolph while I sat in the back awaiting my turn to speak.

When the police learned of the abuse, read the texts on Dolph's phone and even got statements of Britney's abuse, it was declared self-defense, and I wasn't charged with shit. I was let go and the female office who made me her top concern assisted in getting me into therapy. Also, I was gearing up to speak at some Domestic Violence conferences in the future. Ding dong, the evil that lurked was no longer and the weight being lifted meant everything to me.

Big Mama didn't want to even want to send her grandson off with a funeral because of everything that happened, but after other family members convincing her otherwise, she did anyway. She felt for all my losses and encouraged I speak out so people knew who the real Randolph Farrow was. Yeah, he was 'that nigga' in the hood, but he wasn't shit really but a narcis- sistic faggot who needed professional help a long time ago. He'd taken so much from me and now that he was finally gone, I just wanted to get some closure and move the fuck on.

I had my mother cremated since I had no plans to stay in Boston. She would come with me wherever I was and despite how our relationship turned out, I would always keep her in my heart. Her death hit me hard and if it weren't for Gotti, I truly don't know how I would have pulled through. He survived his gunshot wound to the stomach and was released from the hospital after a week. Dolph died from two gunshot wounds to the lung, but the autopsy report revealed his ass would have died from the drugs in his system as well. He was on coke, molly and percs, plus they found THC. He was really an abusive, out of control fiend whose time was numbered anyway. It was a win-win.

As I looked at the faces staring back at me waiting for me to finish, my eyes landed on Gotti and he winked at me. Mac clutched Britney's shoulder as she smiled and waved at me.

"*You got this*," she mouthed.

Clearing my throat, I continued. "I've heard all the wonderful things everybody shared today about Randolph. I'm just wondering how many of you knew him on a deeper level." I glanced around the church. "I mean, have you ever looked alive but on the inside, were slowly dying? Yeah, me either. Have you ever met someone who promised they were different than the rest, but it was all lies? Have you ever hoped for the best for someone, but they end up bringing out the worst in you? Talk about turn tables. Have you ever ignored the red flags because you thought you were tripping? It wasn't all in your head. Have you ever shared a home with someone, the one place you call a sanctuary, and it no longer feel like a home? More like hell on Earth. Have you ever heard the words "I Love You" but didn't feel the love? It was just all talk."

As I read my poem, I could tell I was connecting to some of the women in the crowd. I was sure they were admirers of Dolph and just waiting to take my place. I tried to hide my disgust at the thought of that as I took the microphone from the stand.

"Have you ever looked someone in their eyes and told them their actions are hurting you? Over and over again. Have you ever had someone treat sex like it was a chore and punishment for you? Just call it modern day slavery. Have you ever gone to bed mad at the world yet sleeping with the enemy causing you this anger? It's sickening. Have you ever laid in the shower letting the water run down, silently crying to God to help you escape this misery? You're not alone. Have you ever missed out on sleep from your mind racing over an argument with someone where you think you might've been in the wrong? They made you feel that way. Have you ever been shamed for being right, forcefully held down and spit on like an animal? It's a shame. Have you ever tried to walk away from someone and been told they'll never let you go? And they mean it."

My eyes shot to the white casket beside me as I heard the cameras clicking. The church was so silent; I had everyone's attention without a doubt. With each word I spoke, I felt like a huge weight was being lifted off my shoulders.

"Take your time girl!" Someone hollered out and a few others clapped.

"Have you ever woken up and reality smacked you in the face? Have you ever said you're really done and mean it this time? Have you ever wanted to break free of the mental and emotional abuse because you finally see that you deserve better? You're so worth it. Have you ever begged God to help you through this journey? Prayer works."

"Amen, sister!"

Looking over at Gotti who stared back at me lovingly, I said, "Have you ever felt yourself slowly coming out of your cage? Have you ever felt the sun really hit you in the face? It feels good. Have you ever smiled for the first time and actually mean it? It's a beautiful sight. Have you ever felt brave enough to share your story? I have."

I wiped a tear that slid down my cheek and placed the microphone back before stepping down. People clapped and hollered for me as I walked over to the front pew. Kase sat there stone-faced, hugged up with some Barbie sitting next to Snookie who couldn't even look my way. I paid them no mind as I reached for Big Mama.

"Are you okay?"

She pulled me in for a hug. "I'm so proud of you and happy all at the same time. Don't you worry about old me."

"Thank you, Big Mama. I'll call you to check on you later," I whispered to her then kissed her cheek.

Gotti slipped his hand into mine. Britney and Mac followed behind us as we left the church. Bitches rolled their eyes and whispered at us, but nobody gave a fuck, especially me. I was free and not even looking back. Just like always, God got me.

"Tahiry, wait up."

I turned at the sound of my name and made eye contact with Jalika. Letting out a chuckle, I shook my head, eyeballing her from head to toe.

"This is the chick I was telling you about," Britney said to me, giving me a look that said she was ready for whatever.

As badly as I wanted to drag her ass, I knew I couldn't with her being pregnant and all. I turned to Gotti and said, "I'll be in the car in a second."

He gave Jalika a look then kissed my lips. "You sure?"

"Yeah, I'm good."

"We right here if anything, sis." Mac nodded at me and sparked up the blunt as they all walked off.

Turning my attention back to Jalika, I squinted my eyes about to say something when she cut me off. "Lemme explain."

"You don't have to."

"Please..." she pleaded. I sighed and shrugged my shoulders then she continued. "I was hurt when you just dissed me for Dolph."

"So you fuck his boy then his brother?"

"It wasn't like that. You know Kase wasn't feeling me. I just wanted to be happy too. You seemed so fucking happy and I was jealous. I wanted that too. I got pissed and cut you off," Jalika explained.

"Yeah, well I'm sure you know that everything glitters isn't gold. Didn't you tell me that shit?" I rolled my eyes at her. "You pushed me away and then come back around, fucking with the same muthafuckas you was warning my ass about. Why? Wasn't you eating pussy last year?"

Crying, she replied, "I broke up with my girl and moved back here. One night I bumped into Snookie at the club and... shit just happened."

"You didn't think to hit me up, Jalika?! You was my best fucking friend!"

"Too much time has passed! We been fell off, Ty!"

"Well, you got what you wanted right? You're happy, right?" I asked her and turned to walk away. Jalika grabbed me by the hand.

"No, I'm not. I'm fucking miserable and lonely. I'm sorry, Ty. I'm sorry you went through so much when we stopped talking. If I could take that day back, I would."

Shaking my head, I told her, "That's neither here nor there. I'm at peace now. We ain't got no beef, I just don't wanna fuck with you."

Jalika's mouth dropped. "What? I mean, we can still be friends. My baby shower got postponed but-"

"Girl, I don't care about none of that." I patted her shoulder. "I wish you best of luck but you know...niggas of a feather, remember?" Walking away, I slipped my black sunglasses over my eyes and hopped into the passenger seat of Gotti's car.

"We out?" Britney hollered. She was riding shotgun in Mac's whip. "You good?"

Looking over at Gotti who smiled back at me, I leaned over and said, "Never better!"

One Month Later

"Yo', you're a trip. You ain't 'bouta ruin my surprise. Turn around."

"You better not be on no weirdo shit…I'll scream…"

"Shut up. Bring your ass on." Gotti hopped out of the car and came around to help me out. Holding my hand, he said, "Aight, you ready?"

"I guess so…"

"Surprise."

Gotti took the blindfold off and my mouth dropped. Limitless Recording Studio was staring me in the face. "What the… no, you didn't."

He laughed. "Yeah, I did. Come on."

"Wait. You was dead ass serious, Gotti? You really started a record label? Like, no cap? All jokes aside?" I asked him question after question, in complete disbelief.

"Yes, love. And I bought this studio. Everything is all me. Come on, lemme show you around."

Walking into an actual recording studio like the ones you seen in movies or on TV was surreal. Pictures of celebrities hung on the walls, the telephones were ringing off the hook and everybody we walked past knew Gotti. *Lemme find out this is really his record label!* Men, women, black, Spanish and white folks were amongst the people who either waved, hugged or dapped him up like he was really and truly that nigga.

"Gotti, how's everything, boss man?"

"Everything Gucci, Shanelle."

"Yo' Gotti. I got a mixtape for you. Some Dorchester kids. I'mma leave it on your desk, cool?"

"Aight, Julio."

"Hey, Gotti. Where were you for Angie Vee's party the other night? It was lit!"

"My fault, Mari. You know a nigga be caught up sometimes. Send her some flowers from me, aight?"

"I got you. Later!"

I was speechless. It was unbelievable. Gotti's whole demeanor changed and it was like he went from a street thug to a businessman with just the snap of a finger. He walked with finesse and confidence beamed off of him. He held onto my hand as we stepped onto the elevator, and I just stared up at him. I tried to appear cool but my shock and amazement was written all over my face.

He laughed. "What's that face for?"

"You're joking, right?" I frowned at him like *nigga please.* "Gotti, you the man! Damn. How do you keep this lifestyle a secret?"

"Not a secret. Niggas know I get down with whatever, but my passion is music. I told you, I ain't gon' let the drug shit affect my goals. I did my time, even served some time and got the fuck outta the game. Music is most definitely my passion but don't sleep on me." He winked at me. "I never hesitate to push a nigga's wig back."

We both started laughing but little did he know, he'd just turned me on. I guess looks really were deceiving because at first glance, with no conversation at all, one would take Gotti for just another thug. Nah, this was a grown ass man on his grind and you had to respect it.

Nodding my head, I told him, "That's what's up. Tell me more. I wanna know everything."

Gotti held me by the waist and whispered in my ear, "You really wanna know everything, huh? Well, this is a start and I have another surprise for you."

The elevator dinged, letting us knew we'd reached the fourth floor. As we walked down the hall, we passed studios with folks in live sessions doing their thing. When we reached Studio E, the weed smoke and smell of liquor hit my nose. Rap music played and there was a young dude waiting on the couch with this chick sitting on his lap, rubbing on his dick.

"Bredo, what's good?" Gotti shook his head. He became instantly annoyed and you could tell ol' boy felt it too because he pushed shorty off of his lap with the quickness.

"Aight, sweetheart. I'mma get with you later. I got shit to do, aight?" He shoved her towards the door.

"Damn, Bredo. Wait, I thought you said-"

"I'mma call you." He slammed the door and turned to face Gotti. "Gotti, my nig. What's the word? Who's the pretty lady?" He grinned and gave him a brotherly dap.

Gotti rubbed his chin and motioned for me to sit down in the chair at the audio workstation. He barked, "Ayo, Bredo. Don't fuck with me! The fuck I told you about having bitches up in the studio, nigga. This is business! You can fuck with them hoes on your own fucking time. Let that be the last time I catch you fucking up. We clear?"

Bredo twisted his lips up and nodded his head. "Yeah, we good, man."

"Aight. This is my lady, Tahiry. Tahiry, this is my artist

Brendon, better known as Bredo."

"Nice to meet you." I smiled and shook his hand.

"Likewise. So this is the chick you was telling me about over the phone, G?"

"Yeah. Her voice is everything. I think she'd be perfect on the track."

"Whoa..." I held my hand up. "Say what now?"

Bredo clapped and rubbed his hands like Birdman. He was grinning from ear to ear when he said, "Aww, shit, lemme go on up in the booth. Play that shit, Gotti!"

"I got you."

"Gotti, what you up to?"

He took a seat next to me and pulled me closer to him. "Surprise. I'mma add you to Bredo's next single. This shit is lit as fuck and gon' get crazy airtime on the radio. You with it?"

"Whaaaat? Oh hellllll nah. Uh, uh... I can't." I stood up and he stopped me from walking away.

"What's the problem? What you scared of? I heard you singing the other night." Gotti cupped my face and looked at me intently. "You got the voice, Tahiry. I'm telling you. Trust me on this."

"Gotti, I've never taken this shit seriously!"

"Well, shit I do! And I'll be damned if I let you push that shit to the side. You deserve this shit. Who knows where it could take you?" I sighed and held my head in my hands and he took them from me to hold. He asked, "I gave you some time to get your emotions together but the time is now. Do you believe me?"

I looked over at Bredo all set and ready to go in the booth.

My eyes traveled back up to Gotti's. Biting my bottom lip, I shook my head and replied, "I guess so."

He started cheesing and kissed the shit out of me. "Aight. Let's make this shit happen. This joint's called *All For You*."

He hit some switches on the workstation and the music began to play. The beat was dope and I could picture people bobbing their heads to it, driving down the street or in the club. It was a love song but with a raw, hip hop feel. Bredo started rapping over the beat then Gotti took a seat and pulled me into his lap.

Holding up a notepad, he told me, "I wrote this hook last night. Sing this shit."

I nervously chuckled. "Just... sing it?"

"Nah." He touched my belly and said, "Sing from here. Sing like you wrote this shit yourself. Sing like your heart is in it. Feel me?"

Nodding my head, I took a deep breath. "Okay." I cleared my throat, closed my eyes and let the words flow.

"This ain't no regular smegular kinda shit.

Baby boy, it's not a game.

I'm tryna have your last name.

The way that you make me feel.

I'm praying it is for real.

Tell me that you feel the same.

Now baby, are you down for me, down for me?

'Cause baby, I'm down for you, down for you.

Please tell me that you're all for me, all for me.

'Cause baby, I'm all for you, all for you."

"Damn, Tahiry!" I opened my eyes to find Gotti staring at me like he wanted to eat me alive. He flashed a smile and said, "Come here, girl." He kissed me so deeply, I swear a bitch got lightheaded.

I dropped the notepad and some more shit as I gripped the back of his head. We started tongue wrestling and our breathing became heavy. The warmth of his tongue was inviting and invigorating. I couldn't pull away. It felt too good. I think we both forgot Bredo was in the studio until Gotti picked me up, sat me on top of the audio workstation and the music stopped playing. I broke off the kiss.

"Aye, y'all niggas forgot I was in here?" Bredo came out of the booth laughing his ass off. "I'mma go take a smoke break. Can we lay this track when I get back?" He smirked at us as he left out of the studio.

"Maybe we should-"

"Bring them lips back," Gotti demanded and pulled me into him.

I couldn't front. My body was yearning for some affection. With my lips against his, I asked, "Would it be wrong if I asked you to fuck the shit outta me right now?"

"Fucks no." Gotti picked me up and we started kissing again all crazy and shit as he carried me over to the couch. I fumbled for the zipper on his jeans while he kissed and sucked on my neck. "Damn, I can't wait to feel you cumming on my dick."

I released the beast from his boxers as Gotti raised my dress above my hips and slid my panties to the side. I thought to myself, *Goddamn this nigga got a lot of dick!* Dolph was average and the only dick I'd ever experienced, so I believed it to be good when I was into it, but this shit right here was definitely about to be a whole different type of vibe. My pussy was wet with anticipation. As soon as he slid up in it, my walls locked him down.

"Mmmm..." I moaned.

"Goddamn..." Gotti groaned in my ear. "So this is what heaven is like?" I couldn't even say shit. His slow yet deep strokes had me stuck. He lifted my ass off the couch and pulled me into him then started drilling my shit. I was moaned so loudly, he covered my lips with his to cease that. "You feel that dick?"

"Oh, my God. Yessss..." I whispered back with my eyes closed.

Maybe he was right. Maybe this was heaven. Gotti did exactly what I asked. He proceeded to fuck the shit out of me. He had me moaning like crazy with tears in my eyes. I felt like all the tension my body held was being released on this nigga's dick. It was everything. The way he moaned my name and had me screaming his was crazy. I just knew people in the building could hear us, but fuck it, he was the boss. My body went into convulsions as I came long and hard. Gotti pulled out and I could tell I shocked the shit out of him when I pushed him back to swallow every drop. I'd never done that shit before, but something came over me and I wanted to taste him.

He threw his head back and groaned loudly, "Fuck dawg..." I sucked him into another nut as he caressed my back. I smiled up at him and tapped me on the thigh. "You some kinda different. I swear." He kissed me.

Giggling, I replied, "Come on before Bredo comes back to lay this track."

"You really with it?" He asked me as we both adjusted our clothes.

"Yeah. I mean, you're right. Who knows where this shit could really take me? After all the bullshit and having someone tell me lies about the very thing you're doing for me, how could

I not give it a shot? This just might be what I need to... I don't know... start over." I wrapped my arms around his neck. "Thank you so much for being good to me. I appreciate you so much."

Gotti kissed my lips and slapped my ass. "I told you, I got you. Now tell me that you're all for me, all for me..." We both started laughing and got ready to handle business.

He called Bredo back into the studio and after about an hour and a half later, Gotti replayed the song. I was floored with how professional I sounded! Like whoa, that was really me singing! Get the fuck out of here! You would have never guessed it was my first time recording a song or even being in a studio. The shit came so natural once I stepped into the booth. Gotti and Bredo were amped as hell. I just sat back all smiles for once and truly happy about the possibilities to come.

THE END

NEED MORE DOPE READS BY TASHA MARIE?

Catch this *SNEAK PEEK* of the

next release dropping!

IT'S A RERELEASE YOU'LL DEFINITELY WANT TO READ AGAIN! Revamped & waiting to be read by YOU.

Giving My All To A Certified Boss

A few feet back, Finesse sat there staring me down. I walked over and took a seat next to him. Buckling myself in, I could feel his eyes burning a hole in the side of my head. After several minutes, the jet took off and I turned to look at him. "Aren't you gon' say something? Do I get a "hi" at least?" I was nice as shit and I'd hoped he didn't realize I was high too.

His jaw clenched and he licked his lips still staring at me. He was quiet then out of nowhere he got up and walked towards the back of the jet. I didn't know if I was supposed to follow him or not but I did. We ended up in this dope ass all black bathroom. I mean, even the toilet was black! As soon as I closed the door behind me, Finesse pinned me up against it with my arms above my head and kissed the shit out of me. Those familiar chills shot up my spine.

"Don't ever pull no shit like that again, understood?" He whispered in my ear holding me tightly in his arms. I couldn't front. I missed his scent! "We both grown as fuck, Melody. Whatever you feeling, don't hold that shit back. I want you to be able to express anything to me."

I wrapped my arms around his neck and passionately kissed him, sucking on his bottom lip. "Finesse, I ain't never had no shit like this before. Plus, you got a girl. I'm scared to let myself get wrapped up in you." I truthfully told him. "You know what I just went through with my ex and here I am fucking with you and you got someone else."

"I get it, ma. I do. But trust me, that shit's dead." He told me. "We can take this shit slow. Let this time away with me show you who I am. Let your guard down. I'm ready to settle down and be all about you if you're with me." He winked at me.

I smiled back. "How are you so sure I'm the one to settle down with?"

"I just know." He pressed his forehead against mine and frowned. "And what I say about you smoking?" I was busted!

Next thing I knew, Finesse was on his knees with one of my legs up over his shoulders devouring my pussy. I guess this was my punishment. The jet was cruising but it felt like the earth was moving when I came all in his mouth. I couldn't even stand up straight. He just laughed at me and unbuckled his pants. He bent me over the sink, slipped on a condom and plunged into my wetness. "Mmmm, I missed this tight pussy." He gripped my waist putting his thumbs in my back dimples and planted kisses along my spine, which caused me to arch my back even more.

I threw my ass back and moaned. "I missed you, too." In a matter of seconds, I could feel myself cumming.

Finesse put my leg up on the toilet seat, which allowed him to go deeper. He was hitting my spot relentlessly. I was thinking to myself, *damn this nigga really tryna punish me.* "You ain't gonna run away from me again, right?" He asked, slapping my ass. I couldn't even speak, nothing but moans escaped my lips. He reached down and did that little thing I love, toying with my clit. "You don't hear me talking to you, dimples?"

I cried out, in ecstasy, "Yes, Finesse, I hear you. I hear you." Now I actually had tears in my eyes. He filled every inch of me. I definitely missed his ass. "I'm sorry." I gripped the sink as I felt myself cumming again. It was becoming hard for me to hold myself up.

His strokes became faster and deeper as he held firmly onto my waist. "Fuck!" He groaned. We exploded together. The best quickie ever. We fixed ourselves and I wrapped my arms around his neck.

I told him, "Don't ever play with my emotions and don't lie to me. That's all I ask. If you're really done being a hoe out here, be done. Keep it one hundred with me at all times. Even if you think I can't handle it. Let me be the judge of that."

He flashed his winning smile. "I got you, ma. For real. All I want you to do is let a nigga in. Trust me."

Made in the USA
Middletown, DE
30 January 2023

23469530R00106